G
N

God's Way Not Ours

Sermons on Isaiah 1

D. M. Lloyd-Jones

THE BANNER OF TRUTH TRUST

THE BANNER OF TRUTH TRUST
3 Murrayfield Road, Edinburgh EH12 6EL

*

© Lady Elizabeth Catherwood and Mrs Ann Beatt 1998
First published 1998
ISBN 0 85151 753 6

*

Typeset in 12 on 13 Sabon
by Watermark
Cromer NR27 9HL
and printed in Finland by
W. S. O. Y.

Publisher's Foreword

These sermons on Isaiah 1:1–18 were preached in Westminster Chapel, London between 3 February and 7 April 1963. They are a fine example of preaching evangelistically from a *consecutive*[1] passage of the Old Testament – in three important respects.

First, although they are firmly based on the meaning of the Scripture text in its original (eighth century B.C.) setting, they are not overloaded with historical and exegetical detail. The larger themes of Isaiah's message to the people of his own day are kept in view.

Secondly, these sermons are pervaded by the conviction and the reality that any passage of Scripture is God's word for all time. They therefore speak to the sixties – an age in which people were slipping their moorings to God's truth and embarking on the open sea of free thinking and free living – and also to the end of this century when their children have landed in a 'far country'.

Thirdly, these sermons focus on the unchanging, recurring needs of human beings and the everlasting good news of God's grace. They deal with the reality of sin as disobedience to God's law, as rebellion, perversity, corruption, ignorance, guilt and condemnation, but exult in the tenderness and abundance of God's salvation, pardon and cleansing through the life and death of Jesus Christ, the incarnate Son of God.

The Publisher
Edinburgh, May 1998

---

[1] *Old Testament Evangelistic Sermons* (Edinburgh: Banner of Truth, 1995) contains sermons on isolated texts.

Contents

*

1: *God Has Spoken*

*

The vision of Isaiah the son of Amoz, which he saw concerning Judah and Jerusalem in the days of Uzziah, Jotham, Ahaz, and Hezekiah, kings of Judah. Hear, O heavens, and give ear, O earth: for the Lord hath spoken, I have nourished and brought up children, and they have rebelled against me. Isaiah 1:1–2

These are the words with which the prophet Isaiah opens this great book of prophecy. It is probably a collection of prophecies delivered at different times, but they form one complete whole.

Why did Isaiah ever write? Why did he speak? The answer is because his people – these people who lived in Judah and in Jerusalem in the days of kings Uzziah, Jotham, Ahaz and Hezekiah – were in trouble. He wrote because things had gone wrong with them and worse things were still to come. It was the situation that called forth the message, and Isaiah wrote in order that he might explain the cause of the trouble and the only way out of it. There is really only one great message in the whole book, though it is a long one of some sixty-six chapters, and here in this first chapter Isaiah gives us a summary of it all.

Now that is the sort of thing one does in speaking, in giving a lecture and in preaching. You also find it very often in the overtures to musical compositions where the opening music gives you some suggestion of the themes that will be taken up and developed. In the same way, this prophet, in this introduction, gives us a clear outline of his entire message. He shows the cause of the troubles, the false ways in which people were trying to deal with them and get out of them, and then announces the true and only way of deliverance.

That, then, is the essential picture, but there is just one other element that constantly appears and I must call attention to it. The prophet Isaiah, as I shall show you, was one of the true prophets of God; but there were other prophets. Israel, in trouble, was always being addressed by two types of prophet. There were the prophets whose messages were given them by the Lord, but there were others also, and the true prophets make constant reference to them as 'the false prophets'. These false prophets were always there, and there were invariably more of them.

The first great prophet, in many ways, was Elijah. The famous story about Elijah on Mount Carmel is typical of the role of the prophet. There stood this one man, Elijah, and opposed to him were 850 false prophets! That is the sort of ratio you always find – one man standing for God and for truth; 850 on the other side.

> *Truth for ever on the scaffold,*
> *Wrong for ever on the throne!*
> James Russell Lowell

Many of the prophets were subjected to grievous persecution; everything possible was done to silence them. Nevertheless, they went on, in a minority and sometimes entirely on their own. They gave the message of God to the people in spite of all that was being said against them. So it has been in the long story of the human race, so it is still to this day.

Now that is more or less the setting of these verses that we shall now consider. 'That's all right,' someone may say, 'but what on earth has it got to do with me? "The vision of Isaiah the son of Amoz, which he saw concerning Judah and Jerusalem in the days of Uzziah, Jotham, Ahaz, and Hezekiah, kings of Judah" – who are they? I've never heard of them before, and it would make no difference if

I never heard about them again! What has all this got to do with modern men and women, surrounded as they are by the problems and difficulties and trials of living in the world today? What's the value of looking at a bit of ancient history?'

Now that is a perfectly fair question, and the answer, of course, is that what we have here is not peculiar to this chapter and the days of Uzziah, Jotham, Ahaz and Hezekiah. It is the message that you find in the Bible from beginning to end. I am never tired of pointing that out, and it is essential that I should. The fact is that it is the word of God that we are preaching and not the word of man. The great message of the Bible from the moment that man fell, right down until the very end, is summarized perfectly here in this first chapter of Isaiah.

'But,' you say, 'all that is about the children of Israel.'

Yes, it is, and let us understand, therefore, how we approach it and why we should be doing so. The children of Israel, about whom we read so much in the Old Testament, were a kind of specimen nation, a specimen people. God chose them; he made them for himself. There they stood among all the other nations. God had dealings with them, and the prophets spoke and wrote in particular to them. Isaiah wrote to the nation of Judah, and to the people of Jerusalem, the capital city.

But, you see, what was true of the children of Israel is true of the entire human race. That is what I mean by saying that they were a kind of specimen people. God made this nation for himself in order that he might speak through them and do certain other things through them. Yes, but God also made humanity; he made the world. His message to the sinful Israelites at this particular juncture in history is therefore the message of God to the whole of the human race in its trouble and distress. It always has been the message – that is the extraordinary thing about it.

[3]

'But,' someone may object, 'not only am I not interested in that chapter of yours, I'm not interested in the whole of the Bible. It is a book that was finished before the end of the first century and here we are now in the twentieth century, so how can it possibly be relevant?'

The answer is that the Bible is relevant because it is a book that deals with men and women in their relationship to God, and that never changes but has always been constant, ever since man first fell. So as you read any part of the Bible, you do not feel that you are merely dealing with ancient history, but with very contemporary history. I shall show that the children of Israel, at the particular point when Isaiah addressed them, were in exactly the same position as the human race at this moment, and that what was true of that nation is true of every individual. So even though it is old, the word of God is ever new since it deals with something that is left entirely untouched by all the advances of knowledge, by all the changes in history, and by all the developments that have taken place in the long story of the human race.

Now I make all that clear in order that you may see the relevance of this message, and as I unfold it, it will become increasingly plain. Here is the picture then: there were the people of Judah and Jerusalem in trouble, in difficulties. They had had a wonderful history, and a great record, but now they had reached the stage when things were beginning to go wrong and problems were arising. Various theories were being put to the people. The suggestion was being made that if they did this activity or followed that teacher, all would be well. So they tried it and all was not well! But at the same time, this other message was coming through the prophets who were raised up by God.

Yet some in Jerusalem were at ease, just eating and drinking and having a good time! You find all this described in great detail by Isaiah, and by Jeremiah and others. There were people who said that there was

[4]

nothing wrong: 'Peace, peace; when there is no peace' (*Jer.* 6:14). Others were taking it more seriously and were trying to find their way out of all the confusion.

And is the world not exactly the same at this very moment? It is in trouble and pain; it is in confusion and is full of conflicting, babel voices. What is the matter with it? What is the matter with each of us? Why is life a problem and a struggle for everybody? Why are we all in difficulties? Why is there so much failure, so much unhappiness? Those are the great basic questions for every individual and for the entire human race. And it is because this message, which we have in Isaiah, speaks to that condition that I am calling your attention to it.

What, then, does this prophet tell us? Now to begin with, we must look at Isaiah's introduction because it is vitally important, and the first thing that he tells us is the reason why we should listen to his message. As we have seen, many people today ask, 'Why should I read the Bible? Why should I listen to preaching? I've plenty of things to read – books on politics, on philosophy, on psychology and sociology. I'm reading them because I'm concerned about the human predicament that you have described. I'm aware that things are wrong, that there is trouble, and I'm trying to come to an understanding. But these books are up to date, written by modern men and women. Why do you ask us to go back and consider that old book?'

That is the attitude of so many. They feel that the Christian message is some sort of anachronism in this modern world, and that, because of its antiquity, it cannot possibly have anything to say that is relevant to our modern situation or worthy of our attention.

Now the prophet deals with that very question. There were people like that in his time; there have always been people like that. So let us follow his reasoning as he explains why we should pay attention to what he has to say. In other words, what is Isaiah's authority? What right had this man first to address his people and then to record his message? Let me put it much more simply and directly. What right have I to stand in a pulpit? Is this sheer arrogance? Am I standing here to say that I know better than most people, and that as the result of my thinking and meditation I know that this, and this alone, is right? But that is not the position of the prophet at all. He tells us why he speaks. He gives us the basis and the grounds of his authority. He tells his nation, his contemporaries, why they should listen to him; and his reasons are equally applicable to us today.

Isaiah states that his words should be heeded because they are not his own. He is not giving expression to his own thoughts or propounding his own theories. He is not setting himself up as a man who is unusually clever or has rare understanding. He is not a man who has applied his mind to the problem and, as the result of much meditation and study, has at last seen a way out and is putting forward his proposition. That is not his attitude at all! Neither is it the attitude of any one of the true prophets.

No, the first two words in the entire book, you notice, are, 'The vision'. Now we must be careful with this word 'vision'. Here it actually means prophecy, 'the prophetic message of'. The word is a technical term. As I shall show, the prophetic message which is here described as a 'vision' has a very special character. The book of Isaiah is one of the books of the Old Testament which come in the category of 'the books of the prophets', and the prophets were a special class of person who claimed to be in a unique position because of what had happened to them.

So Isaiah says that his book is a vision. It is not, he says, the result of his investigation; it is not that he has set up a working party. A royal commission has not been studying the situation, with the chairman now issuing his report! It is a vision – 'The vision of Isaiah the son of Amoz'. The man says, 'I am a prophet.'

And then, to make it quite clear, lest there still be any

confusion, Isaiah says specifically in the second verse, 'The Lord hath spoken.' Isaiah disclaims any particular wisdom or insight. He says in effect, 'I am nothing but a mouthpiece.' John the Baptist said the same, quoting this man's very words: 'The voice of one crying in the wilderness . . .' (*Matt.* 3:3; *Isa.* 40:3). Isaiah is merely a vehicle, a channel; he is an instrument, and nothing more. He says: I am but a voice who is speaking what the Lord has spoken to me.

Now this is clearly basic in our whole approach to Isaiah's message. If you regard him simply as a man putting forward his theories, then, of course, you are entitled to take up an attitude of criticism, you can rightly say that his words are out of date. But Isaiah denies that. 'The Lord hath spoken,' he says. 'This that I am putting before you is a vision.' And in its essence – I am not going into the technical details – this means that a message has been given to him. He is receptive; he does not initiate it.

Sometimes the message was given to these prophets by means of an actual vision as happened later to Isaiah himself. He tells us about it at the beginning of chapter 6:

In the year that king Uzziah died I saw also the Lord sitting upon a throne, high and lifted up, and his train filled the temple. Above it stood the seraphims: each one had six wings; with twain he covered his face, and with twain he covered his feet, and with twain he did fly. And one cried unto another, and said, Holy, holy, holy, is the Lord of hosts: the whole earth is full of his glory. And the posts of the door moved at the voice of him that cried, and the house was filled with smoke. Then said I, Woe is me! for I am undone; because I am a man of unclean lips, and I dwell in the midst of a people of unclean lips: for mine eyes have seen the King, the Lord of hosts.

Now that is a vision.

You and I, it is true, do not know much about visions, and I do not say that we should seek them, but there are such things. This old world of ours is a visible, a seen, a material world, but there is another world, a spiritual world. Say what you like against the spiritists, and I do say that they are wrong, but they are right in this respect – they know that there is another realm. The Bible teaches that there are evil spirits surrounding this visible world. Yes, but the Bible says that there is also the Holy Spirit; there is God and there is the unseen where God dwells. He is Spirit and sometimes, in order to give people a message, in order to give them certainty, God in his grace gives them a glimpse into the unseen realm that they may know the reality of it and speak with authority.

Let us not forget visions. This world has become self-centred and materialistic, and the main trouble is that men and women do not really believe in the unseen. But it is there and every one of us will eventually go into it and know that it is real. We shall know that Christ, the Son of God, came out of that unseen into this world in order to give us this message.

Isaiah looked into heaven in his vision. But he does not tell us that God's word came to him like that at the beginning. God has other ways of speaking to his servants. He speaks also in the depths of the spirit. He gives people understanding and a knowledge of truth; and that is what we mean by revelation. The writers of the Bible never claim that *they* discovered anything. They say that it was revealed to them. God can enlighten people. He can quicken their minds. He can enable them to see through the fog and the cloud of rival theories and confusion. He can give them clarity of understanding. And God generally dealt with the prophets in that way, giving them a kind of divine afflatus. They were taken hold of by the Spirit of God and given insight and knowledge. Sometimes the message came to them unexpectedly, but at other times they may have prepared themselves for it in some way. We need not be concerned about the details – all I am concerned to emphasize is that all the prophets in the Old Testament say together, as Isaiah says here: The vision, the message, the prophecy, the revelation came. God spoke to me, and told me to speak to you.

The last of the prophets was John the Baptist and what we are told about him is this: 'Now in the fifteenth year of the reign of Tiberius Caesar . . . the word of God came unto John the son of Zacharias in the wilderness' (*Luke* 3:1–2). There he was, leading that austere, ascetic life, clothed with camel's hair and a leather girdle, eating nothing but locusts and wild honey, a man meditating upon the things of God. From his mother's womb he had been set apart for this work, and he was seeking the face of God, but suddenly the word of God came to him and he began to speak.

Here, then, is the claim of the prophet and that is why he asks us to listen to what he has to say. That is how Isaiah confronted his contemporaries. That is why he stepped forth and said, 'Listen to this!' And I, too, have no authority whatsoever as a preacher apart from that. God forbid that anything about my method or my preaching or my message should give anybody a vestige of a reason for saying, 'That man is simply putting his own ideas forward.' No, I am nothing but a mouthpiece. I am simply here to unfold the Bible, to let it speak. Why? Because it is the voice of God; it is the word of God; it is the vision, the revelation, of God to his servants. Here it is once and for ever, the message that is needed by the world today as much as it was needed by the contemporaries of the prophet Isaiah.

'But,' says someone, 'that is all very well. That is a great claim to make and, of course, it is the sort of claim all dictators have made. They say, "Listen to me. I, and I alone, know!" Can this claim of the prophets be substantiated? Can Isaiah's claim that this is a vision be proved? Can it be demonstrated? On what grounds do you assert that this is a message from God?'

Well, the very character of the message, in and of itself, is almost sufficient to do that. There is a sublimity about it that you will never find anywhere else. I commend to you the reading of this book of Isaiah. Read it, look at its style and the beauty of its language, but, even more, notice the exalted character of the thought, and the pictures it gives us of God and his holiness and majesty. There is nothing more elevated than the book of Isaiah, and, indeed, of the Bible as a whole, with its style, its subject matter, the thoughts it puts before us and the way it handles them.

If we had no other reason for believing that the Bible is the word of God, that would be quite enough. There are other great books, of course – the works of Shakespeare, for example. But put them by the side of this, and though Shakespeare's language and pictures are marvellous, and though his dramatic intensity is sometimes almost over-whelming, his plays cannot for a moment compare with the sublimity of the Bible's concepts, the way in which it lifts one up and conveys a sense of God.

Then there is another powerful argument for listening to the Bible. Although the prophets wrote, as they tell us, at different times, sometimes separated from one another by quite long periods, yet they all say the same thing. That is quite astounding. They were very different men. Isaiah was a very able man, a man of the court, a friend of kings. Jewish tradition says that he came from the nobility. Jeremiah, on the other hand, was from a priestly family. You can hardly imagine two more differ-ent men. Then Amos was nothing but a herdsman and a cultivator of sycamore fig trees. Yet they all have the same message. Why? Because they all received their message from the same source; in every case it was a revelation. It is not the genius of Isaiah, nor his brilliant poetry, that give his words their power and importance. No, it is the revelation of God. Isaiah spoke and wrote by the power of the Spirit.

God can use anybody. He is not dependent upon man, and he uses these different instruments and causes them all to write the same thing. That is why I am emphasizing that in the whole of the Bible there is only one real message: the condition of men and women in their relationship to God. And there is only one answer to the world's problems, and it is given here, from Genesis to Revelation. Different styles, different forms, different aspects, contemporary allusions, do not make the slightest difference. This great line that runs right through, the one message, the only message, is in every book of the Bible.

Then we must note again the historical element, and this is a very powerful argument for listening to Isaiah's words. In Isaiah's prophecy there is a good deal of prediction; he looks ahead and tells his nation, literally and actually, what is going to happen. And this is the test of a prophet's authenticity. What these prophets predicted was actually fulfilled. Here is one of the early prophets saying to the nation: Though you are God's people, you will be conquered by a pagan enemy. He will sack your city and you will be carried away into captivity. Isaiah prophesied that long before it happened, and it seemed utterly ridiculous at the time. But it did literally happen. Furthermore, Isaiah predicted that the people would be brought back from captivity; and they were.

Now I put it to you, as intelligent people, that this is something you cannot dismiss. Here is foresight; here is a *fore*telling, as well as a *forth*telling. The prophets not only dealt with the immediate situation, they took it further. They looked at the remote future, and as they predicted and prophesied, so it literally came to pass. The supreme example of this is their prophetic utterances concerning the coming of the Lord Jesus Christ into this world. What is chapter 53 of Isaiah's prophecy but a detailed description of the cross on Calvary's hill, 800 years before it happened?

Then the last reason, of course, that we adduce as an argument for believing the prophets is the abiding character of the message – in spite of the passage of the centuries. As we follow Isaiah in his diagnosis of the condition of his people, we might very well think that he is living today! The situation he portrays is still true, the trouble is the same. He says: Listen, this is not merely a contemporary message, it is the message of God for the condition of humanity at all times and in all places.

So that is Isaiah's first point; that is the reason why we should listen to his vision – 'The Lord hath spoken.' I pause for a moment to ask a simple question: Do you get the feeling, as you consider this message, that you are meeting with God and that God is speaking to you? I make no claims to knowledge; I do not know any more than anybody else. I believe this word because it tells me the truth about myself; it tells me the truth about the whole world. It is the only hope I know of. It is God speaking. So realize, as you listen, that you are listening to what God is saying through a humble instrument who is not worthy of a moment's consideration.

The second thing Isaiah says is this: Listen. Listen to what I have to tell you. What is it that Isaiah has to tell us? Well, his first proposition is that, in the whole universe, the human condition is something phenomenal. The condition of the world, of every one of us at this moment, is a monstrosity. Had you ever realized that? Listen to the way in which Isaiah puts it: 'Hear, O heavens, and give ear, O earth.' He is calling upon heaven and earth to witness, and by this he does not mean the angels and human beings but the literal, physical heavens and the actual, material earth. And he calls them to witness, to look at men and women – 'Hear, O heavens, and give ear, O earth: for the Lord hath spoken.' Look at this, says the prophet. Earth, heaven, listen. Look. This is what God says, 'I have nourished and brought up children, and they have rebelled against me.'

Isaiah, let me remind you, is addressing inanimate nature and later on he will bring in the ass and the ox. He asks, in effect, 'Are you not amazed at men and women? Are you not amazed at what they have become? You stars,' he says, 'you are behaving as you were meant to behave. You are obeying the laws of your nature. You are moving in your orbits and you never miss your time; you are always at the right moment and always keep everything to the second. Earth, you are revolving on your axis; you are moving round the sun, and you always do it exactly. You are behaving as you were meant to behave. You are obeying the laws of your own nature and of creation. Wonderful! But look at humanity: it is not doing that.' The heavens and the earth testify against humanity. The regular passing of spring, summer, autumn and winter; the growth of the seed into the bud and the flower; the development of the fruit – this is God at work in creation. But men and women are a mass of contradictions.

We are so proud of our knowledge, are we not? We are so interested in the heavens, outer space, sun, moon, stars and all these great distances. We study the earth and its geology; we know about horticulture, agriculture, growth and all these things. Very well, then, let us accept Isaiah's argument. We are so proud that we have discovered what we call 'the laws of nature'! That is all right; they are there, and they always have been. It has taken us a long time to discover them. All these things in the universe obey the law of their nature; they are doing what God intended them to do. That is why our inventions are possible. All we have done is observe that certain things happen in a certain sequence, and we have gone on to say, 'I can harness this, I can make use of it. If I do this, then that will happen. Very well, I'll try it.' We make our experiments and ultimately our discoveries.

[13]

So these laws of nature are in the heavens and in the earth. Everything behaves as it is meant to behave. Everything except humanity! 'I have nourished and brought up children, and they have rebelled against me.' Men and women are unnatural. In their present condition they are a blot upon the landscape. They are a contradiction in creation; they are in a wrong position; they are not functioning as they were meant to function.

Now that, of course, is the point that the world does not realize. We start with the problem as far as our situation is concerned and set up our committees of investigation, our royal commissions. We are going to examine it! But wait a minute. Before you call any commission, stop and ask this question: Was this world, and our life in it, meant to be what you and I know it to be? Were men and women created in order that they might spend most of their time, and their ingenuity and energy, in inventing infernal machines to kill their fellow human beings? Is that what God intended? God made man and woman at the beginning, and he made woman as a helper for man. He said, 'These two shall be one flesh.' Did God do that in order that they might commit adultery and get divorced? And we could go on and on.

Have you ever faced such questions? It is the beginning of the biblical message, the first thing God has to say to us. He says: This world was never meant to be like this; the story of the human race was never meant to be like this. This is a phenomenon, something astounding – heaven, earth, look at it! Inanimate nature is amazed at men and women. They were meant to be the lords of God's creation, and its crowning feature, and there they are, monstrosities in its midst. That is Isaiah's first proposition. All that we are born into is wrong; the condition of the human race is about as far from what God intended it to be as is conceivable or possible.

Have you realized that? Here is a message that only this book, the Bible, utters to the world today. Everyone else starts with things as they are, and asks how we can make them better. But you will never make them better until you realize that they are all wrong, and have got to be made anew and afresh. You need a new creation, a regeneration. There must be a new beginning.

Then Isaiah's second proposition is that men and women are in this condition entirely and only as the result of their own actions: 'I have nourished and brought up children, and they have rebelled against me.' That is why they are in trouble; that is why they are in a mess; that is why they are alarmed and frightened. They have done it themselves.

Oh, what an honest book this Bible is! What a truthful message we have here! There is nothing that tells us the plain unvarnished truth as the Bible does. Do your newspapers tell you that you are the cause of your own troubles? Of course not! Neither do psychologists and philosophers. No, they do not believe in sin; they believe that men and women are, as they put it, 'more sinned against than sinning'. But the Bible tells us at the very beginning that our troubles are entirely of our own making, that we are where we are because we are fools, because of what we ourselves have done. We are children who have rebelled.

So, then, our troubles are not due to circumstances. The human race and the individual are not in the state they are in today merely because of conditions outside their control. It is not that; it is not some cursed fate.

'But,' asks somebody, 'isn't it the evolutionary law? Isn't it that we are just struggling on our way upwards?'

No, it is not that either. It is that we are on our way downwards. Men and women were never meant to be like this. They were made perfect, and their world was a perfect world. The world is as it is now because of their own deliberate action – rebellion, refusal, a turning away from God. That is the Bible's message.

[15]

And finally, Isaiah puts it like this: the essence of humanity's trouble is 'sin', and he is going on to deal with that. We have here, in the first verse of this first chapter, a masterly analysis of sin. Isaiah gives it to us in detail, for it is only as we understand sin, and see ourselves as sinners, that we have any hope whatsoever of being delivered. The Bible puts repentance before faith. We must go down before we go up. We must admit where we are wrong before we can be put right. We must understand what sin really is.

What, then, is sin? At this point I shall only give the prophet's first indication. Sin is not so much a matter of what we do as of our relationship to God. The trouble with most of us is that we always think of sin in terms of sins that we commit. 'Oh, I mustn't do that,' I say, 'that's sinful.' But there is something more terrible than that, for even if we did nothing wrong at all, our attitude towards God would make us sinners. Sin in its essence is the very thing that the prophet talks of here: it is rebellion, revolt against God, and we must put this first. You may be a very moral person, nobody can point a finger at you, but what is your relationship to God? Sin is rebellion against God; it is self-centredness.

I would put it, therefore, in this way: God made the world, and he made it perfect. He made man and woman and he made them for himself. They were meant to live to the glory of God and to be blessed by him. And we are in trouble, and the whole world is in trouble, because those perfect creatures who were made by God, deliberately rebelled against him. 'I have nourished and brought up children, and they have rebelled against me.' Here is the essence of all our ills.

What is the cause? It is a wrong attitude to God. The devil suggested it – 'Hath God said?' (*Gen*. 3:1). Has God said that you must not eat this? Ah, of course he has because God knows that in the day you eat of that fruit, 'then your eyes shall be opened, and ye shall be as gods, knowing good and evil' (*Gen.* 3:5). The devil said: God wants to keep you down.

And the man and woman believed it. They harboured a wrong idea of God. They believed a lie about him and, having started with this wrong attitude to God, their hearts became bitter against him. They rebelled against him. They said, 'Why shouldn't we do this? The serpent is perfectly right, why shouldn't I assert my will? Why shouldn't I have this knowledge?' So they deliberately asserted their free will and did that which God had told them not to do. That is rebellion. It is saying, 'I'm going to defy that king. I'm going to defy his laws. I'm going to do what I think is right, though it's a blank contradiction of what he has told me.' That is exactly what the man and the woman did.

And that is why our world is as it is at this very moment, and why the only hope for humanity is the message of the Bible. You can give people better houses, shorter working hours, and higher wages. You can multiply your entertainments – radio, television, books. You can give people food and clothing, educate their minds, give them all they ask for. But, as long as they are basically rebels against God, their world will remain as it is today. 'Thou hast made us for Thyself and our hearts are restless until they find rest in Thee,' said St Augustine.

Men and women, like the heavens and the earth, are meant to obey the God-given laws of their own being. If they do not, there is contradiction and confusion; there is misery, pain, anarchy and chaos. There must be; there always has been; there still is. What Isaiah said eight centuries before the birth of Christ is as true today as it was when he first uttered it: 'Hear, O heavens, and give ear, O earth: for the Lord hath spoken, I have nourished and brought up children, and they have rebelled against me.'

Are you unhappy? Is there a running sore in your soul? Are you fighting a losing battle? Are you for ever seeking happiness which you cannot find and peace which eludes you?

'What's the matter with me?' you ask.

It is that, like everybody else born into this world, you are a rebel against God, and until you acknowledge your folly, until you yield yourself and your life and your all to him who has a right to it, because he made you and because he will judge you, you will never find peace. 'For rebellion is as the sin of witchcraft,' said the prophet Samuel to King Saul (*1 Sam.* 15:23). There is nothing more terrible than to defy God. It is much worse than drunkenness and immorality. Defying God, living your own life, thinking your own thoughts, that is the cause of human troubles. The amazing thing is that life is not worse – in this world, and for the individual. Such conduct deserves punishment and hell.

There is only one explanation of why things are not worse, and it is this: we would receive nothing but hell were it not that God is loving and gracious. Why did he ever give this message to Isaiah? Why did Isaiah have this vision? Why did he ever say, 'The Lord hath spoken'? Was it merely to condemn? No, no. The ultimate object was to save. It was God's love that raised up prophets. God was pleading with the people, exposing their ills and calling them back, calling them to repentance, and assuring them that he has abundant mercy and compassion and a great pardon to give them.

But God did not merely raise up prophets. No, there is more. 'God so loved the world, that he gave his only begotten Son' (*John* 3:16). He did not merely raise up men and give them his messages, he sent his Son from heaven – 'The Word was made flesh, and dwelt among us' (*John* 1:14). The very Son of God left heaven and came on earth in order to deliver us – and in later studies we will look more closely at what this means. So listen, listen to the heavens and the earth as they express their amazement at you. Listen to their message and fall down before God and repent.

2: *Ignorance*

*

> *Hear, O heavens, and give ear, O earth: for the Lord hath spoken, I have nourished and brought up children, and they have rebelled against me. The ox knoweth his owner, and the ass his master's crib: but Israel doth not know, my people doth not consider.*   Isaiah 1:2–3

As we return to these verses at the beginning of Isaiah's prophecy, let me remind you that this is a message to which we must listen because it is from God. It can be divided up into two sections. The first section emphasizes that we must be clear as to why things are as they are, and why we are as we are. Then, and only then, are we in a fit state to listen to the answer and to the solution. I put it like that deliberately for I want to emphasize it. People will not believe the gospel until they see their need of it, so the first thing we must do is establish this need. That is invariably what the Bible does from beginning to end. The Bible says, 'Repent and believe the gospel.' Or, as the apostle Paul reminded the elders of the church at Ephesus, when he was with them he testified to the Jews and also to the Greeks, 'repentance toward God, and faith toward our Lord Jesus Christ' (*Acts* 20:21).

Now some people do not like this first part, the call to repentance. 'Why don't you come to the gospel?' they say. 'Why don't you just offer Christ to the people? Why don't you just tell us what God has to give us in Christ?'

Again, my only answer is that I know full well that nobody will really listen to the gospel until they have seen their need of it. Why do so few of the people around us claim to be Christians? It is because they have never seen any need. Why do they not believe in the Lord Jesus

Christ? Their answer is, 'Who is he? What has he got to give?' They are not interested – 'Couldn't care less,' they say. They regard the Christian faith as something played out, finished, totally irrelevant to life at the present time. So it is no use standing up and saying, 'Come to Jesus.'

'Why should we come to Jesus?' they say. And it is our business to show them why.

That was the whole trouble with the children of Israel. They did not realize that anything was wrong. That is why God sent the prophets. The children of Israel were listening to those false prophets who were saying, 'Peace, peace; when there is no peace' (*Jer.* 6:14). They were 'settled on their lees' (*Zeph.* 1:12); they were 'at ease in Zion' (*Amos* 6:1). They said, 'What are you talking about? Everything is going very well!' So the first thing that was necessary was that Israel should be brought to realize her need.

So in the beginning of this message Isaiah starts with the need, the call to repentance. What, then, is the cause of the trouble? First, as we have seen, it is that men and women are a kind of phenomenon, a monstrosity in the universe, and second that the human race is itself responsible for its present predicament – that is another great message throughout the Bible. And Isaiah's third point is that this trouble that humanity has brought upon itself is entirely due to its sin.

So the next great question is: What is sin? Now we have seen that Isaiah answers that question here in the introduction to his great prophecy. He tells us, in the first instance, that sin is rebellion, revolt against God – 'I have brought up children, and they have rebelled against me.' We have seen, too, that sin is not primarily a matter of actions and of deeds. The really serious thing about sin is that it denotes a wrong attitude towards God. That is what makes people sinners, and therefore Isaiah puts that first. People are prepared to admit that they are not perfect. 'I'm not a perfect saint, you know,' they say. As if

[20]

anybody thought they were! But that is not the point. What they are really saying is, 'Ah, well, I know I do certain things that are wrong.' But how different that is from admitting that their real trouble is their wrong relationship to God!

One man actually told me that. He used to attend my church, and he had realized the point. He did not mind my condemning particular sins, he knew he was guilty of them. What he could not stand was hearing me say that quite apart from what he did, he was a sinner, that he was in the wrong relationship to God. He was ready to improve himself, but he did not like the idea that he needed to be born again.

But that does not end the matter, unfortunately. The question that immediately arises from Isaiah's words at the end of the second verse is: What makes people rebel against God? Why did the first man and woman rebel against him? And the answer is given us here in abundance. We begin with Isaiah's statement in verse 3: 'The ox knoweth his owner, and the ass his master's crib: but Israel doth not know, my people doth not consider.' Let me put it to you in the form of a number of principles.

The first principle is this: What is sin? Sin is rebellion, as we have seen, but secondly, sin is that which blinds our minds, and leads to ignorance and a failure to think. That is what Isaiah is telling us. 'Israel doth not know, my people doth not consider.' This is a most important matter. This is the great case that the Bible makes against the whole of humanity as it is by nature, and by its fall from God. What makes men and women rebel against God? It is sin, and what does sin do? It stops people thinking. The main trouble in the world at this moment is that men and women are ignorant and refuse to think; and the message of God through the prophet is a call to stop and to think and to reason.

Of course, I know full well that this must sound ridiculous to many people because the common idea about

Christianity is that it is based entirely upon the failure to think. Ask, 'Why are most people outside Christianity today?' and you will be told, 'Oh, because they are intelligent people! They are thinkers! They are reasoning people who use their minds! They are not interested in that sob stuff that is doled out in chapels and churches. They have long since seen through the dope, the opiate of the people. They study science and face the facts! And those miserable people who still go to places of worship and sing hymns, oh, they just lull themselves to sleep; they are emotionalists, feeble people who don't use their brains, if they have any!'

That is the common notion, is it not? That is why most young people cease to go to Sunday school when they reach the so-called 'problem adolescent years'. They are now adults. They have grown up and are going to think! They took religion before because they could not resist, they swallowed it without understanding, but now, 'When I became a man, I put away childish things' (*1 Cor.* 13:11)! That is what they think. And yet the whole message here, as everywhere else in the Bible, is that the facts are the exact opposite, and the whole trouble with people is that they are as they are because they do *not* think; they do not reason; they are ignorant.

There are many statements of this in the Bible. Let me give you some by the apostle Paul. Take what he says about himself, for instance. I do not suppose that Christianity has ever had an abler and more bitter opponent than it had in Saul of Tarsus, who afterwards became the apostle Paul. He hated it; he reviled it; he thought he was doing God a service by trying to exterminate it. But then his eyes were opened and, looking back, this is what he wrote: 'And I thank Christ Jesus our Lord, who hath enabled me, for that he counted me faithful, putting me into the ministry; who was before a blasphemer, and a persecutor, and injurious' (*1 Tim.* 1:12–13). Why was Paul like that? He continues in verse 13, 'but I obtained mercy, because I did it ignorantly, in unbelief.' In effect, he is saying, 'When I was persecuting Christ, when I was blaspheming his name, when I was trying to exterminate Christianity, and the Christian Church, I was ignorant. My whole trouble was that I acted in unbelief.' But, of course, he had thought he was very clever; he had thought that he was right, that he was doing God's work. He had thought that as a Pharisee he had understanding and these so-called 'followers of the Way' were to be dismissed off the face of the earth. But later he wrote to Timothy, 'I did it ignorantly.'

Paul says the same about everybody else. He writes to the Corinthians, 'But if our gospel be hid, it is hid to them that are lost: in whom the god of this world hath blinded the minds of them which believe not, lest the light of the glorious gospel of Christ . . .' (*2 Cor.* 4:3–4). Ignorant! They cannot think! Again he says, 'But we speak the wisdom of God in a mystery, even the hidden wisdom, which God ordained before the world unto our glory: which none of the princes of this world knew: for had they known it, they would not have crucified the Lord of glory' (*1 Cor.* 2:7–8). They looked at Jesus Christ, the Son of God, and said, 'A carpenter! A blasphemer! Away with him!' They did not recognize him.

This ignorance was not only true of the Jews, it was equally true of the Greeks. And, says Paul, there is only one explanation – a veil was over their minds. They were blinded by the god of this world, thinking they knew, yet not knowing. They were incapable of reasoning and were blinded by prejudice, preconceived notions and ideas.

Let me give you one other statement of Paul's which is still plainer: 'This I say therefore, and testify in the Lord, that ye henceforth walk not as other Gentiles walk, in the vanity of their mind, having the understanding darkened, being alienated from the life of God through the ignorance that is in them, because of the blindness of their heart: who being past feeling have given themselves over

[23]

unto lasciviousness, to work all uncleanness with greedi-
ness' (*Eph.* 4:17–19). There it is. That is why people do
not believe the gospel; that is why the world is as it is.

How many of the masses of the people who think they
are clever by not being Christians have ever read the
Bible? How many even know what the Bible teaches? Ask
them what they think Christianity is, and you will be
amazed at their ignorance. It is a failure to *think*. So the
Bible calls us to think. It asks us to stop and listen to this
message.

What is the message? It is a revelation. A revelation of
what? It is a revelation of truth. Oh, I do want to make
this plain and clear! It seems to me to be tragic that people
should be outside the blessing of salvation largely because
they have this foolish, ignorant notion of Christianity,
determined only by prejudice – this idea that it is just a
feeling or an experience. Of course, there are people who
come seeking experiences, who are not interested in
anything but just feeling happy, but if this is your view,
then you are going to be disappointed. This message to
men and women conveys the *truth*. The apostle Paul
makes this perfectly plain. He says that we should pray
for all types and kinds of men. Why? For this reason:
'. . . God our Saviour; who will have all men to be saved,
and to come unto the knowledge of the truth' (*1 Tim.*
2:3–4).

The purpose of preaching is to bring people to a *knowledge of the truth*. Paul was given that commission by the
Lord on the road to Damascus. Our Lord said in effect, 'I
want to make you a witness and a minister. I want you to
go to the people, and to the Gentiles "to turn them from
darkness to light, and from the power of Satan unto
God" (*Acts* 26:18). I want you to open their eyes as I
opened your eyes. Now they are in ignorance and they
cannot think. I want you to go and make them think.'

This message, you see, is primarily a matter of teaching.
That is why, if I may say in passing, whatever else you

may accuse me of, you cannot accuse me of entertaining you. I am ready to enter into a competition. Take the time you spend paying attention to what I am saying, and then compare it with the way other people spend the same amount of time. During which period of time do you find thinking and reasoning going on?

Some people say to me, 'Look here, you're overtaxing your congregations. They can't take it!'

Why can't you take it? It is because you cannot think! The whole world is sitting back and being entertained, being made to laugh. It is all so easy. You press a button and it is all done for you. Does that make you think? Does that make you reason? You are being lulled to sleep. Think of the entertainment provided by the Sunday papers, and the other media – they are stopping people from thinking! And so the world goes from bad to worse and we are amazed that we have problems. No, Christianity is not first and foremost an experience; it is truth. Truth leads to experience. 'God be thanked,' says the apostle Paul to the Romans, 'that ye were the servants of sin, but ye have obeyed from the heart that form of doctrine which was delivered to you' (*Rom.* 6:17).

This is a revelation of truth, says Isaiah. The first thing I am calling upon you to do is to stop for a moment to think, and to reason, to consider your position and why you are in it, and then to listen to the way to get out of it.

Then the second principle, the second reason why people rebel against God, the second effect of sin, is that it perverts men and women and makes fools of them. In revolt against God, they think they are clever, but actually they are making fools of themselves. They are behaving in a very stupid manner. The psalmist said, 'The fool hath said in his heart, There is no God' (*Psa.* 14:1). Now 'fool' there means not only an ignorant person but someone who does not realize his position and obstinately refuses to consider it. A fool is someone who is in a most a most precarious position, but says, 'I'm all right. Everything is going well!' Fools will not stop and listen; they reject it all. You say, 'That man is nothing but a fool.' There's nothing else to say about him. He is deluding himself and he refuses to be told.

Listen to Isaiah's words: 'The ox knoweth his owner, and the ass his master's crib: but Israel doth not know, my people doth not consider.' Why do you think Isaiah chose the ox and the ass? The answer, of course, is that of all the animals, they are the most stupid. Of all the creatures in the universe they are the most obstinate and difficult to handle.

So Isaiah chose the ox and ass to make his point. Even the ox and the ass know their owner and their master's crib. Dull and stupid as they are, they have an instinct that makes them recognize their master. It is very difficult to drive an ox; an ass seems sometimes almost immovable. You can pull and push and beat an ass and he will not move, but when he is hungry and sees his master coming with the bucket, he rushes towards him immediately! The ox and ass obey their instincts: they want the food, and have observed the one who brings it. They seem so dull and stupid and unobservant, so lacking in any response to any kind of persuasion, but when it becomes a matter of food and sustenance, they at once obey the law of their being and rush to get it. But men and women do not! They are bigger fools than an ox or an ass!

But, further, it is not folly merely, it is actually a question of perversion; men and women are unnatural. The ox and the ass are perfectly natural. They may have a stupid nature, but the instinct of self-preservation, the instinct of having their hunger satisfied, operates and puts them right at that point. They remember, they know, they observe and act. But human beings do not. They who were made lords of creation behave in a manner that is perverted and unnatural; they deny the law of their own being.

How is this? Well, all men and women who have ever

lived have always had within them a sense of God and of eternity. Archaeologists, who may not be Christians themselves, have been able to show conclusively that even the most primitive races of people have a belief in an ultimate, supreme God. Archaeological findings support this truth which the Bible has always taught. Of course, I know that many people spend most of their lives trying to prove that there is no God. That is how they try to silence this sense, this feeling and instinct, that there is a some-one, something, higher and greater than themselves. The ancient Greeks had this feeling. They built their temples to Zeus, Artemis and Apollo, and then among them was an altar 'to the unknown god' (*Acts* 17:23). They could not give him a name, but they knew he was there – a god, a power.

Every human being feels instinctively that we are not made for this world. Longfellow's words, 'Dust thou art, to dust returnest,' were not spoken of the soul. God has placed eternity in our souls and in our hearts. We cannot imagine ourselves coming to an end.

'Oh,' you may say, 'I don't believe that we go on after we are dead.'

But I am not asking you what you believe, I am asking you what your instinct is, and your instinct tells you that you are going on. It is an instinct of the being of God, and of the fact that this is not the only life. You have an instinct of eternity.

But men and women, instead of obeying this instinct, as the ox and ass obey their instinct, deliberately fight against it. They try to shake it off, to disprove it, and they think they are clever in doing so. They argue and reason against it. Yet it is there and they cannot stifle it, and so they are in a perpetual conflict. That is why they are more idiotic than the beasts, more stupid than the ox or the ass.

More than that, and still more shameful, men and women delight and glory in that which is the opposite of this instinct. All people have a sense of right and wrong within them, but modern men and women delight in stifling the sense of right, and glory in wrong and evil. I need not give you the evidence because, alas, it is painful and obvious, and is constantly before us all.

It seems to me, as I read the criticisms of most of the film and drama critics at the present time, that if anything is clean it is dismissed as primitive and childish. Nothing is of any interest except that which is foul and perverted and ugly. This is realism; this is real art! And they glory in it – '. . . whose God is their belly, and whose glory is in their shame' (*Phil.* 3:19). They are worse than the ox and the ass. Animals do not do that sort of thing, it is only human beings who do it. They make fools of themselves. They pervert themselves and show their perversion. They violate the law of their own being.

And, finally, men and women reject all teaching and all light that is offered to deliver them. The ox and the ass, however dull and stupid, see the master coming with the bucket and the food and rush to him, but what do men and women do when light is offered to them in their darkness? What do they do when salvation is offered to them in their lost state? They react against it; they refuse it; they speak against it. And they think they are clever in doing so. Our Lord said, 'And this is the condemnation, that light is come into the world, and men loved darkness rather than light, because their deeds were evil' (*John* 3:19). Everything they needed was there before them, but they argued, they resisted, they fought, they threw stones and they crucified him. 'The ox knoweth his owner, and the ass his master's crib: but Israel doth not know, my people doth not consider.' Sin perverts human beings and makes fools of them.

Lastly, let us look for a moment at what men and women do not know, what they are ignorant of as the result of sin. Here is the tragedy. And notice that the prophet emphasizes that this ignorance is about the most important thing of all. The ox and the ass are dull and stupid and they do not know many things, but there is one thing they do know. Try to make the ass go this way and it will not; then try to make it go that way, and it insists on doing the opposite! That is the trouble with the dull, stupid ass. It does not seem able to take your commands, hopeless creature! Ah, yes, but when it becomes a question of food, it does know. In every other thing it does not seem to know the difference between one man and another, and nobody can do anything with it, but let its master come with a bucket of food and at once it recognizes him and rushes to the bin. Why? Because its food is an absolute necessity, it is vital to life. And the tragedy of men and women in sin is that it is just there that they are ignorant. That is where the whole perversion shows – in their ignorance and refusal to think about the one thing that matters.

Sin is very selective. Sin has no objection at all to our knowing anything we may want to know about science, outer space, and atoms. It will encourage us to go in for such knowledge. Philosophy? Certainly! As much as you like. Music? Art? Yes! Now I am not condemning these things. I am just trying to show you the stupidity of sin. The devil has no objection to our studying all these things, and having great knowledge and understanding, and spending a lot of time in meditating upon them and working them out. That is quite all right!

But there is one thing that sin never wants you to know and it is the most important thing of all. It is what the human race is most ignorant about. It is God, and men and women themselves. It is the soul; how to live and die. It is what happens in eternity. That, you see, is where the whole cleverness of sin and of the devil comes in. You are allowed to know as much as you like about many things, but when it comes to this thing that is essential to life and to well-being, the food of the soul, that is where the ignorance comes in.

And that is a complete explanation of the world and

the human race at this moment. In certain ways, we have never known more than we know now. Look at our advanced scientific knowledge, look at our knowledge in other spheres, and yet look at our moral problems! There is a contradiction in the world at this moment – this tremendous advance and yet this retrogression in morals, in life, in living, in true understanding of being and existence, in what really matters, the crib, the food, without which life is really impossible. Let me put it to you in the form of a number of headings.

What is humanity ignorant of? First and foremost it is this: the human race, having turned its back upon God, does not know what it was meant to be. What is man? What is the modern idea of man? Well, you know as well as I do. The modern idea is that he is just a glorified ape, just an animal which has a little more understanding than other animals! Nothing else. That is all he has been reduced to, and people glory in this.

But what in truth is man? Well, listen to the terms. 'I have nourished and brought up children,' says God. What does 'brought up' (or 'raised up') mean? It means made great, given honourable rank. 'Israel' refers to God's chosen people, a people he made for himself that he might enjoy them and that they might enjoy him. 'My people' – and all humanity – at the beginning, were made for that very reason, to be the people of God. God is saying: I have raised up children. I have made them great. I have made them honourable. I have given them a most exalted and wonderful position.

And this is just another way of saying that men and women are essentially souls made in the image of God, meant to be the companions and the friends of God, meant to be sharers in God's glory, meant to be the lords of creation. But they do not know that. They were not made merely to eat and to drink and to indulge in sex, but that is the impression given today. 'Those things alone are wonderful,' people say. 'Let's have more of them – in our novels, on our radio and television programmes. Let's have it everywhere!' They ridicule the things of God and life. They blaspheme God. All humanity once knew – but 'My people do not know, they do not understand.'

The tragedy of the world is that people do not know their own being; they do not know what they were meant to be. God raised them up and gave them honour, mastery and power. They were not meant to die, they were meant for everlasting glory in the presence of God. But, 'Israel doth not know, my people doth not consider.' Do you? Do you realize what you are? Do you realize what you were meant to be, or are you ignorant?

Secondly, people are ignorant of the fact that they are utterly dependent upon God and upon the provision that he makes for them – 'The ox knoweth his owner, and the ass his master's crib.' The ox and ass know they are dependent. They know that if their master does not come with the food, they will starve. Instinct tells them that. But men and women do not seem to know this. They think they are so clever. They can harness the elements, and master the oceans. They have mastered the forces of gravity and put people into outer space. There is nothing they cannot do! They can produce their own food; they are independent of creation.

But read again that great psalm, Psalm 104: 'These wait all upon thee; that thou mayest give them their meat in due season.' Everything in creation – the mountains and the valleys; the springs and the rivers; the animals, the birds, the grass, the flowers – 'These wait all upon thee; that thou mayest give them their meat in due season. That thou givest them they gather: thou openest thine hand, they are filled with good. Thou hidest thy face, they are troubled: thou takest away their breath, they die, and return to their dust. Thou sendest forth thy spirit, they are created: and thou renewest the face of the earth' (verses 27–30). This puts it perfectly. Everything is in the hands of God, and if God were to withdraw his Spirit and his sustaining power, the whole universe would collapse immediately.

Men and women are so clever, yet they do not realize that their life is entirely in the hands of God. Do not forget these little viruses that cause illnesses. They are very small, but they can defeat all our knowledge. This is God's charge against fallen humanity – 'The God in whose hand thy breath is, and whose are all thy ways, hast thou not glorified' (*Dan.* 5:23). God can remove any one of us out of this universe at any moment. What is your life? It is but a breath, but a vapour. What if God withdrew his providential care? You would have no food. You would have no clothing. You would have no health. He can take it away in a fraction of a second. We are absolutely in the hands of almighty God, but we do not know it – 'Israel doth not know, my people doth not consider.'

But, oh, the terrible part of it all and the ultimate tragedy is that men and women are ignorant of the excellencies of the provision which God supplies. Look at your dull ox, your stupid ass. There is the ox, stolid, immovable, it sees the bucket and the food and it rushes for it. The excellencies of the food! It does not know that as a result of reason, nor because it is a dietician. It does not know it because it has made an analysis. It knows because it has eaten. That is experience; it is instinct. But men and women do not realize the excellencies of what God is providing for them, and they are the only creatures in the whole of God's universe that do not. That is why sin makes humanity perverted and unnatural, worse than the beasts and worse than the heavens and the earth.

What is God's provision? It is the great message of the Bible; it is salvation. What does the world need today? What do you need? In the first place, you need to be delivered out of your misery, do you not? You need to have blessing; you need to have abundance. Where can you get it? You can only get it from your Owner, from your Master, from your Maker – God. The ox and the ass recognize the owner and the bucket, but humanity does not recognize God, and God's bucket, which is the Bible. And yet everything the world needs is here – the message of salvation.

And what is this message of salvation? It is the news that you can be delivered out of your troubles by being reconciled with God. That is what you need. All troubles are due to this rebellion which is produced by sin. I must be reconciled, but how? There is only one way – and it is given here: 'God so loved the world, that he gave his only begotten Son, that whosoever believeth in him should not perish, but have everlasting life' (*John* 3:16). You do not pay for the food, it is a free gift of God, it is the grace of God in all its thoroughness and fulness.

Not only that, God will give you new life, a new start, a new outlook and a new mind. He will then feed you with an abundant supply – truth, knowledge, everything you need. He will give you protection against the world and the flesh and the devil and everything that is set against you. Christ has said that he will be with you: 'I will never leave thee, nor forsake thee' (*Heb.* 13:5). In life, in death, whatever happens, he will be with you. He has promised it. He gives food for your soul, knowledge of God, companionship and the certainty of entry into a life of glory and of bliss that baffles description, beyond death and the grave. That is what God supplies in his crib, in his bin. Here it is for you, all you need.

'Your whole trouble,' said Isaiah in effect, uttering the word of God to his contemporaries, 'is this: you do not know your Owner. You do not know your Master. You do not know what he has for you, what he is offering you, what he has mixed in the crib for you. It is because you do not know that you refuse to consider. But come, consider, reason, think, begin to face it. How are you going to die? How are you going to live? How are you going to spend eternity? There is only one answer. There is only one supply that can prepare you for it all. It is all here.'

Come, listen to the message, the reasoned message of God. Listen to the dumb ox, the stupid ass – they are condemning you today. Listen to them, but above all, I say, listen to God and begin to eat.

3: *Going Backwards*

*

Ah sinful nation, a people laden with iniquity, a seed of evil-doers, children that are corrupters: they have forsaken the Lord, they have provoked the Holy One of Israel unto anger, they are gone away backward.   Isaiah 1:4

Rebellion, ignorance, foolishness and perversion are, as we have seen, the general characteristics of this condition called *sin* which is making the world what it is today. People have a curious notion that the gospel and its message are remote. They think that a preacher should be talking politics the whole time. What an utterly shortsighted view that is! The preacher is meant to show you the thing that stands behind politics, behind all social and economic troubles. That is what matters. All human organizations and agencies are failing because they are being handled by men and women who are sinners. You cannot put this world right by politics, or by any other arrangement you may think of. There is only one basic trouble and it is sin.

That is the explanation of why the world is divided into various camps and why countries pile up armaments and why we are faced with the dread of unthinkable possibilities. That is the trouble with the world. It is only in the Bible that you get a true diagnosis; you do not find it in the newspapers or anywhere else. Here and here alone is the radical explanation.

But the prophet does not stop there; he goes on and we must follow him. If you want to be healed in your spirit, if you want to master life, if you want to be able to look into the face of death without fear, then listen earnestly and follow Isaiah who has given us the characteristics of sin. Let us do so now as he leads us on in verse 4 to see some of the things that sin leads to in practice.

Now you notice that the enormity of sin and its base-ness comes out once more and that the prophet's message here is a kind of inevitable consequence of his words in verses 2 and 3. Are you interested in logic? If so, follow the logical process here. See how Isaiah traces out his argument, how one thing leads to another. This is what you may call 'the anatomy of sin'; it is a kind of system, a kind of body. Isaiah starts at the beginning and works it out. You cannot be in this wrong relationship to God without its showing itself in certain ways.

It is interesting to notice the way in which the prophet introduces this next step to us. He puts it before us by means of the word 'Ah' – 'Ah sinful nation'. Isaiah is expressing his sense of wonder and astonishment, his sense of anger and grief, his sense of shame. He looks on at his own nation, remembering who and what they were – Israel, the people of God, the people whom God had made for himself. As God made man and woman at the beginning, he made this nation for himself. He made man out of nothing, and he made this nation, as it were, out of nothing. He took just one man, Abraham, and turned him into a nation. But Isaiah looks on at this nation and what can he do but shake his head and say: 'Ah!' What a tragedy! What a perversion! What an enormity! What a sight!

We have already seen how Isaiah has called heaven and earth to witness to this. We have seen how he has even produced the ox and the ass to express his own amaze-ment. In effect, he is saying: 'Is it possible that the Israel of God should have come to this?' And I can translate that into more general terms for our own times. Isaiah is asking us to consider whether it is possible that men and women, created in the image of God, should be what we see before us in the world today. Yet such is the case. And if you begin to understand these things, if you have any real conception of what Adam and Eve were when they came from the hands of God, and see what their descendants are now, in the depths of their evil and iniquity, there is only one thing to say, and that is 'Ah!' What a terrible thing sin is!

Now let us ask ourselves a question or two as we go along. What is your reaction to the state of the world? Are you astonished at it? What is your reaction to what is going on before your eyes, and is so popular and so acclaimed? Those who have insight and understanding, says Isaiah, are rendered almost speechless. What can they say? They can but hold up their hands in horror. Are we doing that? The whole purpose of the Bible, the whole business of preaching, is to bring us to understand that we must see things as they are, unmasked before us. Our eyes must be opened, and then we will know the same astonishment that possessed the prophet before us.

But what is he astonished at? In the first place, he is astonished at the terrible character of sin and the terrible things it does. We can summarize the lesson of this fourth verse by putting it under three headings – three principles.

Sin, Isaiah says, is that which makes men and women forsake the Lord and go backwards. Sin is that which makes them despise 'the Holy One of Israel', and provoke him to anger. I wonder whether we catch something of the significance of this extraordinary statement? Sin makes people despise the almighty and everlasting God and all that belongs to him.

The world is exactly like the prodigal son. According to our Lord's parable, here was a young man, one of two sons. He was brought up by his father, who was obviously a wonderful man – kind, loving and considerate. The son had a beautiful home, and nothing was ever denied him. But this younger son began to think to himself that this was not so wonderful after all, and neither was his father! He grew tired of that way of life and said, 'I'm getting out of this.' He thought that there was something better in some far country; he had heard stories about it.

'If only you could get there!' he was told. 'This is nothing, you still remain a baby here, under your father's thumb. That's the life!'

And so the son decided to leave. He forsook his father, left his home, and away he went.

That, says Isaiah, is what the children of Israel have done. That is what humanity did. God made the man and woman in his own image and put them in Paradise. God the Father came down and visited them and talked to them, and they had everything they needed. That was their home. They only had to pick the fruit of the garden. They did not have to work for their bread by the sweat of their brow; they did not have to contend with thorns and this-tles and briers. But what men and women did, according to the Bible, and what they persist in doing, is to leave that. They forsake everything that is true of their Father and their home; they despise them.

This, of course, is what people do not realize, but it is taught throughout the Bible. 'The carnal mind,' says the apostle Paul, 'is enmity against God: for it is not subject to the law of God, neither indeed can be' (*Rom.* 8:7). What is 'the carnal mind'? It is self-will; it is forsaking God as a person, and his law, and everything that he stands for. How necessary it is that we should realize this! As we have seen, we are in far too much of a hurry to get on to particular sins, but sin is much more important than sins. There would be no trouble about sins were it not for sin. And the ultimate sin is a wrong attitude towards God.

Men and women were meant to glorify God and to enjoy him. But what are they doing? They are repeating what was done at the beginning when the first man and woman began to question and to listen to the suggestion of the devil: 'Hath God said?' (*Gen.* 3:1). What right has God to say? There you see the wrong attitude to God coming in. Today men and women no longer glorify God. They no longer enjoy God. They have forsaken him.

And, of course, men and women contradict themselves. In sin, and as the result of the fall, they are always so anxious to get to the highest circles, to meet 'the top people', and to get to the very top. They are always clamouring to get to know important people, and yet they have turned their backs upon God, they have forsaken the Holy One of Israel. They have despised the companionship of the Lord of glory; they think they know of someone better! They start like that, with that attitude towards God himself.

And then they also despise God's laws, and God's way of life. God who made us, who in that sense is our father, had planned a certain kind of life for us which was meant to be very happy and holy. Adam and Eve were made upright and innocent. There was no sin in them, no darkness, no evil, no pain, no sorrow. There was nothing unworthy. They were made perfect. They had a righteousness which was the righteousness, as it were, a part of God's own nature in them. And they were meant to live a pure life: no trickery, no chicanery, no backbiting, no jealousy, no envy, nothing dark, nothing hidden, everything open, everything plain, everything pure, everything true, everything noble, everything uplifting. They were meant to live that sort of life and God put them into a position to live it.

That is the home into which the man and woman were born, with the Father in the centre. But they first of all despised their Father, and then they despised the home and everything that it stood for. Instead of living as God had planned, they began to despise these things – and men and women still do. One of their commonest jokes is about the religious life – they call it 'goody-goody' or 'narrow'. The world today is sorry for people who go to church. 'What a tie!' it says. 'Look at them. Fancy doing that!' The world despises Christianity, ridicules it, and

[39]

laughs at it, as it laughs at everything that belongs to God. You see, people begin to put their own ideas in place of God's ideas. 'The carnal [natural] mind is enmity against God: for it is not subject to the law of God, neither indeed can be' (*Rom.* 8:7).

God has given us the Ten Commandments to show us how to live. 'Start by honouring me,' he says in effect, 'and having me as your God. Do not take my name in vain. Do not take my day in vain. Do not kill. Do not steal. Do not commit adultery. Do not bear false witness. That is how I want you to live,' says God.

And men and women say, 'What pleasure is there in living a life like that! Narrow! Not allowed to commit adultery; not allowed to kill people with your mouth; not allowed to denounce people and indulge in backbiting. What a life! Hardly worth living! They despise God and his laws and all his ways, and everything that is characteristic of the home into which God put humanity at the beginning.

So as man forsook God at the beginning and brought calamity upon the whole cosmos, and bequeathed calamity to his progeny, so that is the essence of the trouble in this world today. The world is as it is today because people are still forsaking God and everything that he stands for; forsaking his ways, and doing it deliberately; turning from him; refusing to listen; laughing at his way; walking far away from it. Is that not the whole position that confronts us? Is the world not glorying in its base attitude towards God? Does the world not think that it is clever in ceasing to be religious? Does not every adolescent pass through a phase of thinking that it is wonderful not to believe in God, and that not to keep his laws is the way to find freedom and emancipation? Is that instinct not in all of us? That is the result of sin. We always think we know better. There is always some wonderful country far away – 'a far country'. This church business, this Christianity, this God, belong to the past. Over there is the life. Let's get to it! So God is forsaken, and his whole way, and his love.

Yes, but we are reminded here that such a path is always a going backwards – 'they are gone away backward'. That is the biblical answer to evolution. The world thinks that it is going forward and upward. Never! The world as it goes from God, goes backwards. You go up to God, and if you turn your back on him you are going down, you are going from the supreme Being, the Creator of the ends of the earth, the Holy One of Israel. Turn your back upon him, and you leave his home, you leave the place into which he has put you. You leave his holy laws, and way of life, and you assert – what? Yourself! Your opinion and the opinion of the clever types who write to the papers and appear on the television! You put them before God. Is it surprising that Isaiah says, 'Ah sinful nation'? Madmen! Fools! Leaving God, leaving holiness, leaving heaven, as it were, and following your own devices and desires. So that is the first thing Isaiah tells us here: this terrible thing called sin makes people go backwards.

Then the effect of sin is shown still more clearly in the type of life that it leads to after people have forsaken God. This is the second principle arising from verse 4. Life is a journey. This process of sin is a journey. You leave home first, and then you go somewhere else because you think it is so much better, the prospects are so great there! Well, let us see where you arrive. Let us see what you become. 'Ah sinful nation, a people laden with iniquity, a seed of evildoers, children that are corrupters: they have forsaken the Lord, they have provoked the Holy One of Israel unto anger, they are gone away backward.'

Now the prophet is doing everything he can to open the eyes of his contemporaries. They are in trouble and things are going to get worse but they cannot see that. He preaches to them, others preach to them and remonstrate with them, but still they will not listen. Isaiah says in effect, 'What can I do to make you see what you are doing? Look, here is the picture, that is what you have left. What have you gone to?' And here he paints it before them, and he uses terms which make it quite plain that they enjoy the life they have taken up. Notice what he says. They are a *sinful* nation, a people *laden with iniquity.* That means that they have gone into it thoroughly because they think it really is wonderful; they are absolutely laden. They have not been playing with sin, they have not just skimmed the surface, but are laden with iniquity. And if this does not make us see the enormity and the perversion of sin, what can?

If the world could only see what it is doing, if it could only see what it is gloating over, and enjoying and boasting about, and then consider what it has left for the sake of that, it would repent immediately. And that is what happens to the people who do repent – like the prodigal son, they 'come to themselves'. They see what fools they are and say, 'What am I doing in this far country with the husks and the swine, I, who used to be in my beautiful home?' That is exactly what happens when people are convicted of sin, and repent, and become Christians. But let us see it in the terms which Isaiah uses.

Here is the first thing Isaiah tells us about this life which people take up after they have forsaken God: it is a *sinful* life. We have already given some definitions of sin. Here is a further definition: sin is transgression against divine law or against principles of morality. That is a very good definition. Sin is deliberately breaking God's law. The commandments say, 'Thou shalt not.' Men and women say, 'I will,' and they do. That is sin.

The laws of God are perfectly plain, and there is no need to argue about this. Is there anybody who really wants to defend killing and adultery and all these things? Of course not! The morality even of primitive peoples condemns such things. Yet people deliberately transgress God's law. They look at the law and say, 'There is the law

[42]

of God, there are your Ten Commandments, right, I'll spit on them and then stamp on them.' And they do it deliberately and gloat as they do it.

The next term Isaiah uses is *iniquity* – 'a people laden with iniquity'. Now these terms, of course, are all related. *Iniquity* means unrighteousness, a terrible absence of righteousness. It means what you become when you cease to keep the law. As righteousness is good and upright, this is twisted and perverted. It means wickedness and it leads to gross injustice. And Isaiah says that they are literally laden with iniquity.

Then we come to the word *evil*, which means bad or wicked. This is a terrible analysis, is it not? Is it just the work of a poet with a lively imagination? No, Isaiah is an exact observer, a reporter, a man who has mixed with people and who knows life. He is not sitting in some kind of glass case; he is not ignorant. He says: I know life. That is what I have seen. This is what is true.

Isaiah's last term is in many ways the most terrible of all – 'children that are *corrupters*'. He says: Let's be clear about this. These men, who are sinful and iniquitous and evil, are also corrupters. By that, Isaiah means that they corrupt themselves and they also corrupt others. Had you realized before how up to date the first chapter of the book of Isaiah is? I am almost beginning to think that he was in London yesterday and read all the newspapers and watched some of the television programmes!

What is the meaning of the word 'corrupt'? It means rotten or putrid, something that is decomposing, something that is depraved or debased. It means something that is perverted, that becomes polluted, that festers and begins to disintegrate and smell. The whole thing is a putrid mess – that is corruption. And Isaiah says that humanity, in deliberately turning its back upon God to make this so-called wonderful world and life for itself, has chosen that!

There is a sense in which it is almost unnecessary for

me to comment. The modern world is full of confidence and pride in its achievements. 'How wonderful we are!' people say. 'How ignorant every generation was before us. How ignorant our forefathers were, one hundred years ago! What did they know? Why, what did they know even fifty years ago? Look at the advances we've made! Look at our knowledge! To ask us to believe in God and to believe in righteousness and the Ten Commandments is an absolute insult! We're no longer going to be bound by such childishness. Religion is all right in the infancy of the human race, but not when we've reached adulthood, not when we stand on our own feet, able to reason and understand. Religion is for primitive people, not for us! We need something better and we've entered into a promised land!'

And what is your promised land? Corruption! Look at it round and about you. Look at the corruption of life in almost every walk and department. Is it not about time that we faced the facts? This is not a theoretical matter. Christianity is about life and living and about facts. The Bible is meant to help us to live in this world, and it asks us to face the facts of life. People in the world have left God, they have left the Ten Commandments. They say that they do not need them. They can plan their own life. They can live in their own way. But what have they to show for it? Nothing but sin, iniquity, evil, corruption! The filth of the newspapers; the filth on the television screens; the horrible suggestion, the innuendo, the playing with sex – one of the gifts of God. The twisting and the perverting of it all; the leering and the giggling and the laughter. Corruption! Marriage is laughed at. What is marriage? What is a vow? Why should a man or woman be bound by a pledge? What does it matter if they are suddenly attracted to someone else? Why should they not be?

And, of course, it is all so daring, so wonderful! The look, the glance, the suggestion, the wink! But, oh, the corruption and the foulness! Oh, the loss of everything that is clean and pure and chaste and wholesome and ennobling and uplifting! The men and women who laugh at Christians for reading the Bible or for going to church – that is what they have instead. That is what they think is so wonderful. That is what they are boasting about. That is what they say people should really go in for as they assert themselves and express themselves. Nothing sacred, nothing pure, nothing noble. Everything a joke, everything an object of ridicule, everything clean to be turned off and to be laughed at! No sanctity, no true emotion any longer, but cynicism, suggestion, everything doubted. They are corrupters!

But still worse is the fact that they not only corrupt themselves but also corrupt others and delight in it and boast of it. The apostle Paul puts it in terrifying language at the end of the first chapter of the Epistle to the Romans. If you think the Bible is out of date, you are making a mistake! The popular programmes these days are the programmes that are supposed to mirror life. That is modern art, is it not? We no longer like artists who paint beautiful portraits. 'Ah,' we say, 'that's photographic. Let's see life in the raw, as it is. Oh, what tyros these others are! What mere amateurs!' Do you want to know life as it is? Then you must read Paul's words:

Because that, when they knew God, they glorified him not as God, neither were thankful; but became vain in their imaginations, and their foolish heart was darkened. Professing themselves to be wise, they became fools, and changed the glory of the uncorruptible God into an image made like to corruptible man, and to birds, and fourfooted beasts, and creeping things. Wherefore God also gave them up to uncleanness through the lusts of their own hearts, to dishonour their own bodies between themselves: who changed the truth of God into a lie, and worshipped and served the creature more than the Creator, who is blessed for ever. Amen. For this cause God gave them up unto vile affections: for even their women did change the natural use into that which is against nature: and likewise also the men, leaving the natural use of the woman, burned in their lust one toward another; men with men working that which is unseemly, and receiving in themselves that recompence of their error which was meet. And even as they did not like to retain God in their knowledge, God gave them over to a reprobate mind, to do those things which are not convenient;

And here is the description:

being filled with all unrighteousness, fornication, wickedness, covetousness, maliciousness; full of envy, murder, debate, deceit, malignity; whisperers, backbiters, haters of God, despiteful, proud, boasters, inventors of evil things, disobedient to parents, without understanding, covenantbreakers, without natural affection, implacable, unmerciful: who knowing the judgment of God, that they which commit such things are worthy of death, not only do the same, but have pleasure in them that do them.
(*Rom.* 1:21–32)

The cheering of the silly audience, the tittering and the laughter: they corrupt themselves, yes, but they are not content with that, they want to corrupt everybody else. They are given the opportunity and they think it is clever, and they are applauded. Oh, how corrupt, how vile, how foul, how unclean!

But it is the principle that matters. And the principle is that men and women, in living a life like that, think they have done something wonderful. They have forsaken God, they have turned their backs upon the Holy One of Israel, in order to have that! The son, the prodigal in his father's home, was dissatisfied, so he left. And there he is with the swine, with the husks, penniless, empty, and hopeless.

Have you seen it? Do you still think it is clever not to believe in God? Do you still think it is clever to break the Ten Commandments? Do you still think it is clever to be as unlike Jesus Christ as you possibly can be? Do you think the modern person is really a paragon? May God open your eyes before it is too late. May the Spirit give you wisdom to see yourself as you are. You fool, you corrupter, wake up. Open your eyes and see where your cleverness has landed you, where your forsaking of God has brought you!

Then the last principle from verse 4 is this: sin leaves men and women in utter ignorance and disregard of the consequences to which all this inevitably leads. 'Ah sinful nation, a people laden with iniquity, a seed of evildoers, children that are corrupters: they have forsaken the Lord, they have provoked the Holy One of Israel unto anger.' I would not be a preacher were it not for this. If I had not understood this, I might have been a doctor or a politician, because I think it is the duty of every decent person to do something about the present state of morals in this country. But I am a preacher not only because I am concerned about morals, but because there is something still more serious. Life is bad enough as it is, but the terrible thing is that people do not know where it is all going to lead – *'they have provoked the Holy One of Israel unto anger'*.

Now this is the great message of the Bible, and I must put it before you as solemnly and as simply as I can. Paul says, 'Despisest thou the riches of his [God's] goodness and forbearance and longsuffering: not knowing that the goodness of God leadeth thee to repentance? But after thy hardness and impenitent heart treasurest up unto thyself wrath against the day of wrath and revelation of the righteous judgment of God' (*Rom.* 2:4–5).

The One whom men and women in their wisdom have forsaken is the Lord; he is the Holy One of Israel; he is the Maker, the Judge of the whole world, and he has told us from the very beginning that there is to be a day of judgment. God would not be God if he did not hate sin and manifest his wrath against it. 'God is light, and in him is no darkness at all' (*1 John* 1:5). He made men and women for himself, and they are meant to enjoy him, but they have become what I have described to you, and God in heaven hates it. He has told us so in his messages to Moses and the prophets. He has told it still more plainly in the message through his own beloved Son, our Lord and Saviour Jesus Christ.

Do not listen to the foolish people who say, 'I don't believe in the wrath of God, I believe in the God of Jesus,' but read the words of the Lord Jesus Christ in Luke 17:26–29: 'As it was in the days of Noe' – eating and drinking, marrying and giving in marriage: of course, a typical Saturday night! '. . . Likewise also as it was in the days of Lot' – what were they doing? The same thing, eating, drinking, marrying, and giving in marriage, planting, buying, selling and having a wonderful time! Business was good, there was plenty: Let's have more of it! The joys of Sodom and Gomorrah, the place that Lot chose. Abraham was a fool, of course! He lived on top of the mountain, but Lot had an eye to business, he knew what was what! He wanted some pleasure; he wanted to do well; he chose the cities of the plain.. What a life! 'As it was in the days of Noe . . . and the flood came, and destroyed them all . . . as it was in the days of Lot . . .' – this is our Lord speaking – '. . . even thus shall it be in the day when the Son of man is revealed.'

As certainly as you and I are alive today, every one of us is going to stand before God in the final judgment, and he has told us already that his wrath is upon sin. 'The day of wrath' it is called, when God will show what he thinks of this kind of thing, and the punishment he is going to mete out upon it. It will be the day of the revelation of the righteous judgment of God. God is still there and God always will be there. The world can laugh, the world has often laughed at God. The people before the flood laughed at him; the people of Sodom and Gomorrah laughed at him; the people in the time of Christ mocked the preaching of John the Baptist, ridiculed the preaching of the Lord himself. The world has always done this, but the fact that the world has laughed has not made the slightest difference. What God has said, God has always done. And there is going to be an end to this world. There will be a day of judgment when the righteous judgment of God against sin will be revealed, and be made plain and clear, and everyone will have to stand and be judged.

Now you can say you do not agree. Very well, you prove that it is not true. If you like to risk all that merely on your opinion, I can say no more to you. I am simply here to tell you what God has told me to tell you, and here it is. You will have to stand there and the clever people will have to stand there, too – 'Every eye shall see him' (*Rev.* 1:7). Do not forget that 'one day is with the Lord as a thousand years, and a thousand years as one day' (*2 Pet.* 3:8). God does not belong to time.

You may ask, 'If he's going to do this, why didn't he do it long ago?'

I do not know. All I am telling you is that he will do it: 'Of that day and that hour knoweth no man, no, not the angels which are in heaven, neither the Son, but the Father' (*Mark* 13:32). If you have forsaken God and are living that sinful life, all you are really doing is treasuring up unto yourself 'wrath against the day of wrath and revelation of the righteous judgment of God' (*Rom.* 2:5).

What a terrible thing! Look at a miser – all he wants is to treasure up money. He keeps all those coins; he wants a great pile. And by living that godless life, that life that forsakes God, by putting forward your own opinion, and your own ideas, and your own way of life, you are treasuring up for yourself wrath against the day of wrath. Everything you do is being marked against your account – everything. You are treasuring it up.

'But,' you say, 'I don't believe in God.' All right, that is put down.

'I can do this, nobody will know.' God knows – it is down. You are treasuring it up.

It is all being amassed. The pages are turned and everything that you and I have ever done or thought or imagined is there in the book. 'All things are naked and opened unto the eyes of him with whom we have to do' (*Heb.* 4:13).

Or if you prefer it in another image that is used in the Scripture, it is this: 'Whatsoever a man soweth, that shall he also reap. For he that soweth to his flesh shall of the flesh reap corruption; but he that soweth to the Spirit shall of the Spirit reap life everlasting' (*Gal.* 6:7–8). Now this is an absolute law, it is the law of sowing and reaping. If you sow wheat, you will grow wheat. If you sow oats, you will grow oats. Sow potatoes, you will grow potatoes. Sow to the flesh and you will reap corruption. You cannot help it, you cannot sin without paying for it. You will pay for it partly in this world, and much more in the next. It is being treasured up; it is being accumulated. Your account is kept and there you will suddenly see it and you will be amazed at it.

And what is the end? We are told that God's righteous judgment will be revealed, and God's judgment of sin is eternal punishment. What is this punishment? It is what the Bible calls 'hell'. Hell is a place of torment, a place of suffering, a place of misery. It is a place of evil and of spite and malignity. Do you know what it is? I believe it is some sort of eternal filthy programme, when you have realized at last that the thing is debased, but you have nothing else, and you have to live on that for ever and for ever. The foulness, the vileness. That evil, that debased desecration of everything that is righteous and like God. Those who are in hell fester, shut out from the glory and the purity and the holiness of the life of God and his holy angels and his saints.

There have already been judgments in this world – I have reminded you of some of them. There was a judgment in the Garden of Eden; there was a judgment at the flood; there was a judgment on Sodom and Gomorrah; there was a judgment when the children of Israel were carried into the captivity of Babylon. There was a judgment in 70 A.D. when the nation of Israel was ruined, the very city of Jerusalem brought to rubble and to dust, and the nation cast out among the peoples. There have been judgments in the twentieth century. I believe the two world wars we have already had are nothing but the judgments of God upon human arrogance and pride since the middle of the nineteenth century. And another terrible judgment is threatening us in the form of nuclear warfare. But these are mere prophecies and adumbrations of the final judgment that is to come.

What I am trying to say is that if you are living the kind of life that I have been depicting, you are provoking the Holy One of Israel unto anger; you are putting God against you. That is the terrible and the horrible thing about sin. You are making an enemy of God, the One who made you, the One who made you for himself, and who wanted to be your Father, and who wanted to shower his blessings upon you. Make him angry with you, and his wrath will come upon you. Can you not see it? Look at what you have left. Look where you are! What is this life of yours? What is it leading to? What is it giving you? Where will it end?

The amazing thing to me is that God still speaks to us, but he does. Though the people of Judah were like that, God sent his prophet Isaiah to speak to them. Why?

Because he wanted to deliver them. What is the message? Here it is: Repent. Recognize what you are doing. See the utter folly of it all, the arrogance, the enormity, and repent. Fall at God's feet and ask him, 'Is it still possible for you to pardon me? Is it still possible that you can receive me?'

And he will say to you: 'Yes, I loved you even when you did not know it. I loved you even when you were walking away from me. I loved you even when you spurned me, and ridiculed me, and despised my name and my laws and my home. I loved you with an everlasting love in spite of it all. I sent my Son to die for you, to bear your punishment. Believe in him and I will receive you. I will give you a permanent position in the family. We will have a great feast and the angels of heaven are tuning their harps, ready to sing at the return of one such as yourself.'

4: *The Depth of the Problem*

*

Why should ye be stricken any more? ye will revolt more and more: the whole head is sick, and the whole heart faint. From the sole of the foot even unto the head there is no soundness in it; but wounds, and bruises, and putrifying sores: they have not been closed, neither bound up, neither mollified with ointment.

Isaiah 1:5–6

In our study of the introduction to the prophecy of this great, evangelical prophet Isaiah we have seen that Isaiah's message is also the message of the whole Bible. The Bible is a word addressed by God to the world, to men and women whom he himself has made. The children of Israel are but a representative specimen, and what is said to them can be said to the whole of humanity.

We have seen that the first part of the prophet's message is that men and women must realize the cause of their troubles. Of course, they do not like that; any foolish patient in a doctor's surgery does not like that. We want ease, we want deliverance and happiness, and we cannot be bothered with diagnosis, which takes time and investigation. We want something to stop the pain, but it can be a very bad, even a criminal thing, to stop pain before you know what is causing it. You can be masking something serious. So the prophet here does what the whole Bible does. The Bible insists upon our coming face to face with the cause of our ills, and only then does it tell us about the remedy – the gospel, the way of salvation – which alone can deal with and cure those ills.

Now I am not saying this by way of apology, but by way of exposition. I am going to hold you once more face to face with what Isaiah tells us about sin. We have already looked at this for our last three studies, but we

must continue. I must follow the prophet; I am not here
to give vent to my own ideas and theories, but to expound
the word of God. And as Isaiah goes on with his
diagnosis, probing and revealing the depths of sin, I shall
follow him.

This is something that is necessary for us all. Those
who are believers in the Lord Jesus Christ and members
of the Christian church have just as much need as unbelievers to be brought to the realization of the depth of
sin. Why are God's people so often silent and complacent
at a time like this? Why is it that God's people are not all
pleading with him to send revival into the Church? Why
is it that we are not all begging him to open the windows
of heaven and pour forth his Holy Spirit and do a work in
our midst that will shake the nations? I am afraid that the
majority of Christians are not praying like that. And why
not? There is only one explanation. They have never
realized the depth of the problem.

There is a very real danger that Christian people,
because they are good people who are living a good life,
may know nothing about what is happening in the world
round and about them. Because they do not do certain
things, or do not look at certain things, they are not
aware that they are happening. But we are living in a
society that is disintegrating round us. We are living in a
time of moral collapse, and it is advancing with a terrible
rapidity. Are we aware of that? Do we realize that nothing but a mighty outpouring of God's Spirit is adequate to
deal with it? I am afraid that our tendency is to go on with
our nice services Sunday by Sunday, having happy
fellowship, occasionally making a special effort, perhaps,
but generally feeling that everything is all right. You
would imagine from the religious journals that everything
is fine. They say very little about revival; everything
seems to be going well! But here is society collapsing
before our eyes in a terrible moral muddle, in degradation.

We must realize the truth; we must realize that the

problem is such that nothing but an intervention of God himself can possibly retrieve the situation – nothing short of that will touch it. We have tried everything else, we have been busy and organized, but the position is deteriorating and the problem is appalling! Are God's people aware of this? If they are not, I repeat, it is because they have never realized the truth concerning the depth of sin, as Isaiah expounds it in these verses.

So I say these things to Christian people, but still more to those who are not Christians, to those who reject the gospel of Christ, and then think they are clever, to those who scoff at the Bible and feel it is out of date. I say it because I know that all thinking people are aware of the fact that there is something wrong and are concerned about the situation. They write about it, and discuss it together, but, according to Isaiah, they are hopelessly wrong as to the cause of the trouble. As a result, not only will they not believe the gospel, but everything they are doing will come to nothing.

What, then, is the cause? Again I say that the whole trouble is caused by the failure to understand what the Bible means when it talks about sin. Read the apostle Paul's account in Romans 7. 'This,' he says in effect, 'is what is ruining my life, ruining everything, this sin within me.' And the Bible's case is that sin is in all people and this is the essence of the problem. But the world does not believe that. Recognizing that something is wrong, the world has its own suggestions about how to put things right.

First of all, there is teaching and knowledge. The world still believes that all our troubles are due to our lack of education and that what we need is enlightenment, knowledge, the application of reason and logic, and common sense as well – and then, problem solved! So we must thank God for science and education which are going to help us to see and to know! If only people could be trained to think, they say, and face the facts, then there would be no trouble at all. The difficulties can be sorted out by rationalism. Sometimes, of course, people are ready to include in this knowledge the teaching of Jesus, as they call him. They are prepared to quote the Sermon on the Mount. They say, 'How obviously right and true that is!' And so they bring that in. This view that good teaching is all that is necessary to improve the world is the commonest view of all.

But there is another solution, which is similar. Some say that the problem is a matter of sickness. It is held that nearly all the problems that are troubling people today are nothing but some sort of psychological sickness. When criminals are arraigned before a court and tried for some misdemeanour the comment is made, 'You mustn't call it crime, you mustn't call it sin, it's an illness.' So if you put people in prison you do not make them work, you call in psychiatrists, and you speak kindly and nicely to them because they are sick people. If you only do all that, and explain things to them, and give them a new outlook, and a new teaching, and see that they mix with nice, kind people, you will gradually cure the sickness, and the problems of society and morality will be solved.

Linked with this, is a new view of the nature of punishment. One of the greatest changes that has taken place in this century is in the view of punishment. People used to say that the main function of punishment was to punish – it was punitive. But nowadays that view is very unpopular. We are told that the main business of punishment is to reform – it is remedial. Therefore prisons have become reformatories, where we heal people, and teach them, and introduce them into a new life.

Other people say that we need not be too excited about today's problems. The world is advancing, humanity is improving, and it is purely a question of time before men and women will come into their own. They will see their folly and will slough off all the things that have held them back in the upward reach of the human race. In time, they

[56]

will arrive at a kind of perfection. 'Be patient,' it is said, 'Rome wasn't built in a day and the human race isn't going to be put right in a day.'

Now all these views are based upon the belief that men are women are essentially good, or at any rate, they are not essentially bad. 'Oh,' it is said, 'the Bible talks about sin, and the old preachers used to talk about it, but we have outgrown all that; we know that it is all nonsense.' But the fact is that these approaches have now been tried for a long time, and the point has arrived when we must ask the obvious question: What has it led to? What are the results?

Since the publication in 1859 of Darwin's *On the Origin of Species*, the Bible has been increasingly ignored. The majority of people today have more or less thrown it overboard, and in many places the Church has almost disappeared. People feel they can get on without the Bible, and without the Church. But the question still arises: What of the situation? Why is the world as it is? What is the matter? Why do people reject Christianity and believe these other things? There is only one answer, and that is that people have never realized the depth of the problem. They have never realized the truth of the biblical teaching concerning sin. The message of God through the Bible to the world today is that its problem is so deep, so profound, that nothing and no one but the almighty God himself can deal with it. The Son of God came into the world because the problem of humanity in sin was so terrible that nothing but such an intervention could possibly provide a solution. The law had been given but it did not save. Nothing else can save. The law in that it was 'weak through the flesh' could not save us, so God sent his own Son 'in the likeness of sinful flesh, and for sin' (*Rom.* 8:3).

And it was because they, too, did not realize the depth of the problem that Isaiah wrote as he did to his contemporaries nearly 800 years before the birth of Christ. As we have seen, Isaiah starts off his book with an analysis of sin and we have been looking at the essential character, the nature, of sin, and the things it makes people do. Now we come to a new paragraph. Here, in verse 5, the prophet turns to the consequences of sin and, of course, men and women in sin are as ignorant of its consequences as they are of its character. They are blind to what they are bringing upon themselves. So the prophet addresses them in these words: 'Why should ye be stricken any more?' He says in effect, 'Look at yourselves. Here you are, smitten so much that your whole body is covered with wounds and putrefying sores. You are a mass of festering bruises and still you go on sinning. Do you want more?'

It is very important that we should face up to the consequences of sin, and as we do, we will see still further into its character. First of all, we need to realize the terrible *power* of sin. Let us follow Isaiah as he shows this to us, and we must start with the fact that sin is something which affects the whole of life. Isaiah says, 'The whole head is sick, and the whole heart faint. From the sole of the foot even unto the head there is no soundness in it; but wounds . . .' Now that can be interpreted in two ways. I have already interpreted it to show that the whole body is like that because God has been beating this sinful creature; he has been punishing him until he is black and blue and festering with sores. But it can also be taken in another way, and I believe both are true. These words can be, and are, a perfect description of sin itself.

According to the Bible, sin is not just some slight defect, some negative phase in our evolutionary progress. That is what non-Christians believe. They deny that sin is positive, or that human beings are bad; it is just that they are not as good as they ought to be. But the whole point here, in Isaiah, is that men and women are positively evil in the sense that they are being controlled and mastered by this terrible power. Furthermore, the prophet says that this is something that is true of everybody – 'From the sole of the foot even unto the head there is no soundness in it.' Now commentators are agreed that this is a pictorial way of saying that from the lowest to the highest in the land the people are all guilty; they are all in the same boat; they are all suffering from the same thing. And that, of course, is what the Bible always says about humanity and about human nature. 'There is none righteous, no, not one' (*Rom.* 3:10). 'All have sinned, and come short of the glory of God' (*Rom.* 3:23).

This is important because there are some nice respectable people who say, 'Sin? That doesn't apply to polite society and to cultured, sophisticated people, but to backward peoples and people who live in slums.' No, says the Bible, it is true of all classes. The Bible is not interested in social distinctions. All people are sinners, whatever their birth, whatever their ancestry, or their social position. And it is equally true of all types. Some people say that church-going people have a religious complex. If you have that religious kink, you will be a religious person. If you do not have it, you won't be. It's all right, they say. It doesn't matter. Why should everybody have the same bent? So worship of God and the life of faith are dismissed in terms of psychological divisions.

No, says the Bible, God's commands apply to everybody, whatever the type. And, of course, if we were to make an analysis of any congregation attending a church service, what a variety of types we should find! Some are mercurial, some phlegmatic, some interested in art, some in music, some in mathematics, and so on. But with regard to sin, such differences do not matter at all. Whatever the interests, whatever the temperament, no man or woman who has ever lived has not been a sinner and a failure in some moral respect.

And it is equally true about abilities. Some people are fond of dividing up humanity according to brain power – the able people, the gifted people, the thinkers, the great brains, and the other people who have no brains. 'Ah,' they say, 'of course the people who have no brains are religious! But we have brains – we think!'

No, says the Bible. You are all sinners. And, of course, this can be easily proved. The great philosophers say the same thing about religion as the biggest fool standing at a street corner. They both say, 'There's nothing in it!' The only difference between the two is that the philosopher says it in learned pseudo-scientific language. And the philosopher with his great brain can be as guilty of adultery as any Tom, Dick or Harry.

One touch of nature makes the whole world kin.
Shakespeare, *The Tempest*

And brains or lack of brains, learning or ignorance, make no difference at all. So the most learned, cultured people may be slaves to drink no less than the so-called man in the street. These horrible perversions about which we hear so much, are they confined to one class? Of course not! 'From the sole of the foot even unto the head' all are involved. That is what the Bible says.

I must not stop with this. Not only is it true that no one is immune from sin, it is equally true that the whole of each one of us is involved – head and heart. Sin applies to the whole person, the whole personality – mind, heart and will; body, soul and spirit. Sin is not merely a matter of conduct or will, sin makes us think wrongly – we have already seen that. One of the first things that went wrong when Adam sinned was his mind, and the whole trouble in the world today is that we do not know how to think properly. But our hearts, our feelings, our sensibilities and our desires are equally involved. Our will also is involved; it is paralysed.

The apostle Paul says, 'We know that the law is spiritual: but I am carnal, sold under sin' (*Rom.* 7:11).

[60]

Or, 'I know that in me (that is, in my flesh), dwelleth no good thing' (*Rom.* 7:18). There is no part of us that is right by nature. When man fell, he fell as a whole, every part of him fell. Our bodies were not meant to be as they are, they were meant to be perfect and absolutely beautiful. Everything in us is twisted and perverted; it is a matter of total corruption. 'The whole head is sick, and the whole heart faint.' Sin so affects men and women that no redeeming feature is left. That does not mean to say that all people are as bad as they possibly can be, all the time, and at the same time, but it does mean that with every one of us there is a blight upon our very best, something is tarnished, even in the noblest part of us.

You see the importance of this? These people are saying that all we need is knowledge and information, and training of the mind, as if the heart and will were all right. Others then say that all we need is psychological readjustment. Put the heart right, and the mind will look after itself, the will, too. Will they? And then those who preach morality and good conduct, and address the will only, seem to think the mind and heart are all right. But it is their ignorance that makes them think that. The apostle Paul had discovered it all for himself: He says: No, no, I am a mass of contradictions. 'The good that I would I do not: but the evil which I would not, that I do' (*Rom.* 7:19). I am divided in myself; when my mind seems right something else in the members of my body is dragging me down, and when I put that right, this other has gone wrong. Here I am; where am I? What can I do? 'O wretched man that I am! who shall deliver me?' (*Rom.* 7:24). It is a hopeless business.

There, then, is the first point that is made here by the prophet. He shows that sin is a terrible power that has affected the whole of human life in every respect. But, alas, Isaiah does not stop at that. The next thing he says is that sin is a terrible power that prevents us from learning, even from punishment and suffering – 'Why should ye be

stricken any more?' He says: Why are you asking for
more? You have been whipped; you have been beaten;
you have been chastised with scorpions and you look as if
you are asking for more. Here you are, staggering under
the blows, and still going on with the wrong.

Now this is something that this modern generation
needs to learn. Men and women in sin do not listen to the
teaching which God gives them through his word and
above all through the Lord Jesus Christ. God has given us
the Bible. In the past he sent prophets. He even sent his
own Son into the world. He sent apostles, and he has
raised up preachers. And he has done all this to tell men
and women to believe that here is the way of life and the
way of salvation. He offers them the gospel, but they will
not accept it; they reject it with contempt and scorn.

But there is something even worse than that. As the
result of their rejection of his word and his way of life, his
commandments and his gospel, God punishes people. It
is a great principle throughout the Bible that 'the way of
transgressors is hard' (*Prov.* 13:15). God, as we have
seen, made the first man and woman perfect and put them
into Paradise, but when they sinned God punished them –
as he had told them he would. Whenever people sin they
are always punished, though they do not always recognize
it as such. God has said that he will mete out punishment.
He is doing that, and he will do it on a still bigger scale, as
we have already seen. If you put your finger in the fire,
you will get burned, and just as surely, if you sin against
God's holy commandments, you will pay for it. How
does God punish? One way is through remorse. We have
all known it, have we not – remorse, mental agony, soul
trouble, shame, perhaps actual suffering in the body as
the result of some sin we have committed.

So God had been punishing these children of Israel, but
they continued in their sin. They would not learn from
punishment – 'Why should ye be stricken any more?'
What is the matter with you? I have smitten you in order

to correct you and to pull you up, but you go on, you take no notice.

And this, as I have said, is true of the whole of the human race and of every individual to this day. Take the familiar phrase: 'the morning after the night before' – a violent headache, pains and aches all over the body, and, what is more, a sense of shame and debauchery, a feeling of being unworthy and unclean. But does that stop people? Of course not! You would have thought that once would have been enough, and that having had that awful feeling, they would never do it again, but, no, they go on repeating the experience. Of course, that is only an illustration, but it is true in some shape or form of every sin, and yet people go on sinning.

Look at the world today. Look at the suffering and the trouble; look at the pain and the agony. Look at the millions who have been killed, the bereavement, the sorrow. Look at the ruined lives. Look at it all. We have had world war twice over in one century. But has the lesson been learned? War is madness! Nobody can pretend it is anything else. It is sheer lunacy, and we have suffered and suffered. We read our history books and see that war always brings poverty and starvation; it always brings maimed bodies. It is a terrible thing. But as Hegel said, 'History teaches us that history teaches us nothing.'

Though we suffer, though we have the pain, though we are punished by God, we still go on. Some people think that after a national disaster men and women will reform. 'Surely,' they say, 'when people have had to go through a thing like this, they will be pulled up. They will see the folly of the way they have been living and will come to their senses. They will live a new life. There will be a better land, and a better way of living.'

What utter rubbish! Men and women in the grip of sin never reform as the result of punishment and suffering; that is where they show that they are perverted and foolish. No, the power of sin is so great that it dulls people's memories. Immediately after they have sinned, they are filled with shame and say, 'I can't possibly go through this again – that would be inconceivable.' But by the next morning it does not seem quite so bad; the morning after that, it is still less bad; and in a week's time there was nothing at all wrong with it!

And not only can sin paralyse the memory, it can twist facts; it can manipulate them, and prove anything it likes. Sin can manipulate our reason and vitiate all our argumentation. It will inflame our desires; it will paint beautiful pictures; it will put on rose-coloured spectacles. It will also paralyse the will so that when temptation comes again we forget all about what we felt and do the same thing once more.

There is no need to argue about this. If you do not agree with my exposition of the biblical teaching concerning the power and depth of sin, let me ask you this one question: Why do you keep on doing that thing that gets you down, that thing you are ashamed of? Why do you say, 'I'll never do it again!' and then do it again? Why are you always down? Why are you in this conflict that the apostle Paul speaks of? There is only one answer: the power of sin is greater than your power. Sin is the greatest power in the world, with one exception, and that is the power of God.

Lastly, the terrible power of sin makes us so incorrigible that not only do suffering and teaching not correct and deliver us, they even aggravate our sin and make us sin all the more. 'Ye will revolt more and more.' God says: I am punishing you, but it makes you even worse. What is the matter with you?

And here is the depth of sin. Here we see that sin is 'exceedingly sinful' as the apostle Paul puts it in Romans 7:13. This can be seen in the individual, can it not? There is nothing more tragic in the whole of life than to see a poor fellow going down and down and down into the depths of sin. He suffers himself and he brings suffering upon his loved ones. But not only does that not deliver him, it seems to drive him to desperation so that he does it more and more. Every appeal and every correction makes him worse. He seems to be inflamed by everything that tries to deliver him.

And is that not true of the entire human race? The Bible has great illustrations of this. Just before the flood, there was Noah, a righteous man, building an ark and preaching his message of judgment and of righteousness. Do you know the effect he had upon the unbelievers who heard him? They sinned all the more! The more he preached, the worse they got until 'every imagination of the thoughts of his [man's] heart was only evil continually' (*Gen.* 6:5). It was the same in Sodom and Gomorrah. The righteous Lot was living there, but that made the people worse. In the Bible, before every great judgment, the people seem to become desperately worse and worse. It happened before the captivity of Babylon. It has always happened in the past, and it is happening today.

Men and women are becoming more arrogant in their sin. Every day they flout God; they ridicule him and laugh at him. They turn everything upside down and say, as Milton said in *Paradise Lost*, 'Evil be thou my Good.' They preach it; they enjoy it; they gloat in it; they advertise it; and expose themselves. Madly and obstinately they defy the living God. They reject all his appeals, spurn all his instructions, laugh at all his punishments. They say, 'Let's eat, drink and be merry, for tomorrow we die. It's a short life, so let it be a merry one. Then if we're all going to be blasted into nothing, well, let's get our fill before that happens.' Is that not the argument? Is that not at the back of all this open evil, this arrogant, violent, blasphemous sin that is staring us in the face? The apostle Paul expressed the power of sin once and for ever. He tells us that this was his own experience:

For when we were in the flesh, the motions of sins,

which were by the law, did work in our members to
bring forth fruit unto death . . . Is the law sin? God
forbid. Nay, I had not known sin, but by the law: for
I had not known lust, except the law had said, Thou
shalt not covet. But sin, taking occasion by the
commandment, wrought in me all manner of con-
cupiscence. . . . And the commandment, which was
ordained to life, I found to be unto death. For sin,
taking occasion by the commandment, deceived me,
and by it slew me. Wherefore the law is holy, and the
commandment holy, and just, and good. Was then
that which is good made death unto me? God forbid.
But sin, that it might appear sin, working death in
me by that which is good; that sin by the
commandment might become exceeding sinful.
(Rom. 7:5, 7, 8, 10–13)

'You know,' says Paul in effect, 'I, by nature, as a man
in sin, was as vile as this, that even God's holy law which
was given by God to guide me and correct me in the way
of righteousness and holiness, even that law resulted in
my sinning, because, by telling me not to do a thing, my
desire to do it was inflamed.' 'The motions of sins, which
were by the law, did work in our members to bring forth
fruit unto death' (*Rom.* 7:5). And you will often find that
when you give your children teaching on morality, sin is
being stirred up in them. Human nature is so sinful that
even good clean instruction will do people harm. They
will twist it, feed upon it and gloat over it. Sin twists even
God's law so that it makes us worse than we were before
and kills us.

We know that sin is wrong, but does that keep us from
sinning? Of course not! It drives us to sin. We read books
on sexual morality to do ourselves good. It is a lie. We
read them because we like it, because we are enjoying it,
and at the end, when we have read the book, we are worse

than before. No one has ever been cured of immorality by reading books on the control of sex – never has been, never will be. They make us worse, they putrefy the injury and make the wounds run deeper while the foulness increases. That is because sin is such a terrible power and humanity is its helpless slave. Each of us is enslaved in mind, heart, will, body, soul and spirit.

Is there, then, no hope? Well, if what I have been saying is true, there is only one hope. It is not in us. As we have seen, the power of sin is greater than the power of human beings. We are all living witnesses of that, and the whole world is proving it. No, there is only one hope: it is the power of God, and that is the gospel. 'I am not ashamed of the gospel of Christ,' says Paul to the Romans, 'for it is the power of God unto salvation to every one that believeth' (*Rom.* 1:16). What the world needs is not knowledge; it is not teaching; it is not information; it is not medical treatment; it is not psychotherapy; it is not social progress; it is not punishment, even. It is none of these things.

What men and women need is a new heart, a new nature, a nature that will hate darkness and love the light, instead of loving the darkness and hating the light. They need an entire renovation, and, blessed be the name of God, it is the very thing that God offers in and through our Lord and Saviour Jesus Christ. The Son of God came and took unto himself human nature. He united it to himself in order that he might give us that nature. Why did he come into the world? He came because the power of sin and of the devil was greater than the power of all humanity. He came because he has the power, and he alone. He has defeated the devil, and he can deliver anyone who believes in him from the power of the devil and from the power of sin and evil.

The Son of God came into this world in order that we might be delivered from sin in every respect. From its guilt: he died on the cross to deal with the guilt. From its power: he rose again and sent the Spirit who will come and dwell in us that we may stand up to the devil. 'Resist the devil, and he will flee from you' (*James* 4:7). Christ came to make us more than conquerors. He puts his own divine nature into us, this new nature, this new life. Nothing else will suffice. When we are new people, then we will love God and love his word. We will love his teaching, and have his power within us to lead us, and to direct us day by day.

5: *The Desolation of Sin*

*

*Your country is desolate, your cities are burned with fire: your
land, strangers devour it in your presence, and it is desolate, as
overthrown by strangers. And the daughter of Zion is left as a
cottage in a vineyard, as a lodge in a garden of cucumbers, as a
besieged city.*   Isaiah 1:7–8

We have been seeing how Isaiah makes a very thorough
examination and diagnosis of sin. It is not pleasant to
listen to; it is most uncomfortable. But let me make it
clear before I go any further that if the message of the
Bible has never made you feel uncomfortable, then you
have never heard it at all. So many think that Christianity
is merely something that pats us on the back saying,
'Don't be troubled and worried, everything will soon be
all right.' But that is not Christianity: that is the cults, that
is psychology. Here is a book that probes us and
examines us, that puts the searchlight of the eye of God
upon us and reveals us to ourselves as we are. We begin
to squeal; we begin to shout; we begin to ask it to let us
go . But this searchlight will not let us go. It goes on with
its terrifying and terrible examination until we have
really seen our condition, and the disease has been
exposed. Then, and only then, does it apply the remedy.
And, of course, there is a perfectly good reason for all
this. No one ever comes to Christ until the point of
desperation has been reached. No one really believes the
message of this gospel until everything else has been tried
and found to be a failure. So the right way of bringing
people to Christ is to show them what they are without him,
and that is exactly what Isaiah is doing in this passage.

As we have seen, Isaiah's message here is but a typical
sample of the teaching of the whole Bible. But he puts it in

a very dramatic form which we can easily remember. I am therefore not making a theoretical or academic study of the condition of the children of Israel some eight centuries before the birth of Christ, but calling your attention to these words because they are very up to date. The Bible is a book that speaks to us as we are; it is the only book that really knows us. The people who dabble with the human psyche talk about 'analysis'. Oh, this opening passage in Isaiah is analysis! But it is not just getting us to bring up things from our past – no, as we have said, this puts the eye of God upon our soul and reveals things to us that we were never aware of. And those are the things that bring us low; they are the cause of our ruination. In other words, here before us is a revelation from God.

So we have been following Isaiah from the second verse, where he tells us something about the nature and the character of sin, and then from verse 5 onwards as he begins to tell us about its consequences. In verses 7 and 8 Isaiah puts political, social and economic facts before his readers. He says, 'Your country is desolate, your cities are burned with fire: your land, strangers devour it in your presence, and it is desolate, as overthrown by strangers. And the daughter of Zion [the children of Israel] is left as a cottage in a vineyard, as a lodge in a garden of cucumbers, as a besieged city.'

The reference to a 'cottage' and a 'lodge' is a picture with which the contemporaries of Isaiah were familiar. In their vineyards or fields they used to put up a little kind of shelter for the convenience of workers. We often do that now – you will see on an allotment, for instance, a shed in which people can leave their implements for work, and where sometimes they can even live during a busy season. The prophet uses that as a picture – but with a difference. The vineyard is devastated and so the shelter stands alone; and the same with the lodge among the cucumbers. The figure in both cases conveys the idea of something isolated in the midst of desolation. And that, says Isaiah to the people, is your position.

This is a picture, of course, but it was actually true. It did happen to the children of Israel. Eventually, the city of Jerusalem was destroyed and the whole place razed to the ground. The country was ravaged and became utterly desolate, while the people were carried away to captivity in Babylon. But, of course, the important thing here is the principle that what happens in the physical world is a representation of what happens in the spiritual realm. Now I am not saying that sin does not still lead to material difficulties. I shall not dwell on that now, but let nobody imagine that I am saying that sin does not do physical or economic or social harm, for it does. We all know that sin can make a man or woman a physical wreck, and many a country has gone down and its cities have been literally ruined and sacked because they rebelled against God. But it is still more important to realize what sin does in a spiritual sense, and therefore I have tried to classify the teaching of these two verses under the following headings.

First: sin always leads to misery – 'Your country is desolate.' Notice how Isaiah repeats the word desolate – 'Your country is desolate . . . your land, strangers devour it in your presence, and it is desolate.' Desolation, ruination, misery! We saw this in our last study when we realized that God always punishes sin in one way or another and that, in itself, always leads to misery. But what I want to emphasize now is that sin, in and of itself, because it is what it is, always leads to misery.

Now it is just here that we see the subtlety and clever-ness of sin. If we really knew the truth about sin, we would never have done the things we have done. Then none of us would be miserable and the whole world would not be in its present condition. But sin comes in a most enticing form, and, of course, it always offers 'life', always offers a good time, always offers success, always offers happiness. If it did not, nobody would look at it.

This is all set out so perfectly in the third chapter of Genesis. There is the history of the world in a nutshell, and the explanation of why the world is as it is. There is the only explanation as to why one hears what Wordsworth has called 'the still sad music of humanity' – the groaning, the heartache, the misery, the wretchedness. The world tries to put on a bold face, of course, and a bright appearance, painting itself, decking itself up, saying, 'Oh, how wonderfully happy we are!' But what an artificial happiness! The whole thing is a pretence and a sham; it is all manufactured and worked up.

There were Adam and Eve in Paradise – perfection – not having to work by the sweat of their brows, not having to struggle with nature, not having to fight thorns and thistles, a life of happiness and joy. Why is the world not like that now? There is only one answer. When temptation came to Eve and Adam, did the tempter say, 'Do what I tell you and you will be miserable? Do what I tell you and you will lose everything. You will have pain. You will have to work for your bread and earn your living Of course, he said nothing of the kind! He said in effect, 'This is all right as far as it goes, but after all, this is a very small, a very limited life. What about that great prohibition, the commandment that you are not to eat the fruit of that particular tree? Ah, what fools you are! How dull and stupid! Fancy listening to God! Fancy going on with this religious life! Why, you are not living at all! You do not realize your potential; you do not know what you have got inside you. You are being held in. You are being kept down. God is preventing your really expressing yourselves and rising to the true dignity of your own greatness!

'Listen to me,' the devil said. 'Don't listen to him. If you eat of the fruit of that tree your eyes will be opened. You will be like gods. Nothing will be able to stand before you. You will know as much as God himself. You will have absolute control over yourselves. You will have opened a door and you will have a life of freedom, of joy and happiness. Everything will be at your feet; everything will be under your control, and no longer under his. Look at it! Here it is! So simple!'

And Eve looked at the fruit and she saw that it was very good to look at. It seemed the most marvellous fruit in the Garden in colour, form, and perfection! Of course! If temptation were not attractive, nobody would ever look at it. And that is how sin always comes – beguiling, enticing, bewitching, full of beauty and attraction. Oh, the interest and excitement – always an improvement on what we have. It could be illustrated endlessly. This is the cause of the whole misery in the world today. That fool of a man looks at another woman and says, 'What's my wife by the side of this one!' Is that not it? And this is only one illustration out of a thousand, not to say a million.

'Come along,' says the devil, 'if you will only listen to me you will have a marvellous life.' That is what he always offers, but never what he gives – never! Study Genesis 3: it is an epitome of the story of humanity and the sole explanation of the sorry history of the world, because sin is always followed by disappointment and suffering. It is always followed by remorse and, as we have seen, by fear and unhappiness.

Adam and Eve had dwelt with God. Nothing had pleased them more than when God, as it were, came down and walked with them and talked with them, but after they committed this sin, when they heard his voice in the Garden, they ran and hid, filled with fear and alarm. They were unhappy and did not know what to do. And they discovered a problem in themselves they had never had before. What could they do about their nakedness? The suggestion of the devil that had appeared so attractive, so enticing, so bewitching, so wonderful, simply led to what it always leads to, without a single exception. 'The way of transgressors is hard' (*Prov.* 13:15). The wonderful life that the world is offering to people, telling them to laugh at God and at Christ and at chastity and the morality of the Bible, what has it given? What has it led to? It always leads to misery.

But sin not only leads those who commit it to wretchedness; others are involved also. The whole world is miserable because of sin. 'From whence come wars among you?' asks James (*James* 4:1). Wars are devastating; they bring such unhappiness and desolation. They are the greatest curse the human race has ever known. 'Where do they come from?' And James answers, 'Even of your lusts that war in your members. Ye lust, and have not.' Wars originate in pride and arrogance, in the overweening ambition of certain people and nations. It is all because men and women turned their backs upon God and did not submit to him and to his holy law. I keep on repeating this. If only the whole world and everybody in it submitted to God, we would not have bombs; we would not have weapons. There would be no threat of war. We would be back in Paradise. It is as simple as that. But we are fools; we are attracted by sin. We have this feeling that if we turn our backs upon God, we shall have a marvellous life. But we do not. We do not have it in general, and we do not have it in particular.

What would be the result if you made an analysis of the unhappiness, the wretchedness, the misery and the heartbreak in our cities? What are the causes? We know very well what they are: lust, desire, people trampling things under their feet and saying, 'I want this. I must have it. Why shouldn't I have it? There's something very beautiful about it. I've never seen this before. It's never happened to me like this before.' And so they break their vows and break the laws, gratifying their lust, their desire and their passions. But the suffering! Little children suffering, women suffering, men suffering, whole families suffering. Sin is a weed and a canker. It always leads to desolation. That is an invariable rule because sin is a poison and what is in its nature must come out.

There, then, is the first thing Isaiah tells us, but we must go on. The second thing is that sin always leads to loss. Isaiah says: Your land, the land that belonged to you, has been overthrown and taken over by strangers. They have come in and are devouring your substance in your very presence. You are nothing but miserable, pitiful serfs and slaves in your own country. Look at your cities, the cities you yourselves built and your fathers built, the buildings that you were so proud of. What has the enemy done to them? 'Your cities are burned with fire.' Your land flowing with milk and honey, the land that was so fruitful, on which you lived, and the fruit of which you enjoyed, look at it. What is it now? 'Strangers devour it in your presence, and it is desolate.' They take everything out of it and put nothing back. They do not tend it, they do not till it, they just want the proceeds and they will leave it a barren, desolate, wilderness – 'overthrown by strangers'!

Now the spiritual principle here is simple, and again it is taught everywhere in the Bible. It is that sin is always a total loss. It comes offering us everything, but actually it robs us of everything we have – our cities, our land, taken, ruined, and turned into desolation.

'What do you mean?' asks someone.

My first reason for saying this is that though sin offers us so much, it never gives anything of value to us. Had you ever thought of that? Look at the glittering prizes offered by the world, the world that ridicules Christianity, the world that laughs at religion. What are these prizes? Let us ask a plain question. People say they are not Christians because they are hard-headed business executives, because they think, because they are not going to be carried away or be moved emotionally. They say, 'No, we're thinkers.' Well, let us do a little bit of thinking. Let us have a look at the ledger. Let us call in an accountant and see how it works out for us.

What does the world give you that is of any real value

to you? What has all the entertainment that everyone is so mad about really given you? How much better does it leave you? Sin is like the commodities in advertisements. Wonderful! Look at the colours. Marvellous! But they are nothing. It seemed you had something to get your teeth into, but they are all air, puffed up, and they collapse. What does the world's entertainment give to your mind? What does it give to your spirit? What does it give to your soul? Does it help you to live? Does it uplift your outlook upon life? Does it help you when you are taken ill – when you are desperately ill? It is a mockery and you do not want it. Take everything that the world has to offer you which is opposed to this gospel, and when you analyse it, you will find that you have nothing.

Let me sum it up, then, by using the words of the apostle Paul. Here he is writing to men and women who had been living a sinful life, but are no longer in it: 'When ye were the servants of sin, ye were free from righteousness. What fruit had ye then in those things whereof ye are now ashamed?' (*Rom.* 6:20–21) 'Look here,' says Paul in effect, 'let me take you back across your life. There were things you used to do but you do not do them any longer; you are ashamed of them now. But tell me this: What profit did you have in them, even when you did do them?'

The preacher is not a man who lives in a glass case; he is not someone who is out of this world. Like everybody else, I read my newspapers and sometimes I listen to the radio or watch television, and I notice what is happening. And I get the impression that if you really want 'life', and want to get returns, then the more you drink, the better it is! Drink comes into everything – it is introduced at every point. No two people can meet without having a glass in one hand while they are shaking hands with the other. Alcoholic drink is obviously the thing that makes life, life. But what has this really given you? Well, it seems to me that it has come to this: men and women are so miserable that they have to drug themselves to persuade themselves that they are happy.

'But,' they say, 'you can't have a good night unless you have a drink or two. You can't be convivial. You can't have a really animated conversation. There will never be any brilliance.'

Are you sure? Try going without it! Are men and women so fallen, are they so bereft, so bankrupt, that they have to be drugged, and their highest qualities put out of action, before they can be convivial and pleasant, and speak in an entertaining manner? Has it come to that? No, these things have nothing to give us. Alcohol is not a stimulant, it is a depressant – that is a pharmacological statement, a matter of scientific fact. Alcohol releases that which is most primitive in you by knocking out your highest centres of control. Now that is only an illustration, but it is true of sin in every realm and department.

But we must go beyond that. Sin not only never gives me anything, it always robs me of my most priceless possessions, and this is the most terrible thing about it. Isaiah says: Look at your country. Where are your cities? Where are your buildings? Look at your land. It has become a barren wilderness, and all because of these strangers who have come in and have conquered you and robbed you of everything you have.

Make no mistake, sin always does this. There is a classic example in the parable of the prodigal son, which we looked at earlier. Here is a man who said, 'Give me my share of the goods, I want to go to that far country. I can do better with my money there than I ever can here with you, 'stick-in-the-mud'. You never advance. You never know anything. That far country, that is the place! Give me my share.' Off he went to make a fortune, but in the end he found himself penniless, sharing life with the swine, and eating husks in a field.

Sin always robs us of everything that is best in our possession. What do I mean? Go back again to the beginning. Look at what sin did in that first sin committed by Adam and Eve. They lost the biggest and the best things they had ever had, everything that was most precious. God made man and woman in his own image. He made them with an original righteousness. He made them as his friends. He made them as people who enjoyed God and he put them to live in that wonderful Paradise. He gave them peace; he gave them joy; he gave them hope of eternal glory and of immortality. And in that one act of disobedience and sin the man and woman lost it all. They lost their original righteousness and became sinners. They lost their likeness to God and became more like the beasts. They lost their enjoyment of God and it was replaced, as we have seen, by fear. They lost their peace, their joy and their hope of glory. They lost their home. They were driven out of the Garden to till the ground and to earn their bread by the sweat of their brow in a constant struggle against nature 'red in tooth and claw'. And so they lost everything that was priceless.

And as that happened to Adam and Eve at the beginning, so it is the whole subsequent story of the human race. Look at a little child – he is not perfect. No, we do not believe in the 'Peter Pan' idea, but there is a kind of innocence about a little child, is there not? The little child does not know some of the things that you and I know. There he is, still chaste, still pure, still clean. But time goes on, and as Wordsworth reminds us:

> *Shades of the prison-house begin to close*
> *Upon the growing boy.*

He begins to learn things and to know things which he thinks so wonderful and clever. But he does not know that as he learns them, he is losing something; losing an innocence, losing a purity, losing cleanliness of imagination and thinking. Oh, what a robber sin is! And it robs us of

[78]

the most wonderful, the most beautiful, the best things.

It is sometimes said that the best and the greatest things have been done in the world by young people. There is a sense in which this is true because while people are still young they are hopeful and want to make things better. They believe that things can be made better and they make an effort. As they get a little bit older, and reach middle age, they say, 'Is it worth it? Oh, let's put up with it. Do the best you can. Get the maximum out of it.' As men and women get older they become a little cynical. They become doubtful and put the break on enthusiasm. There is no longer any hopefulness and they grow more and more selfish. 'Ah,' they say, 'he's young, he'll grow up. He'll learn a thing or two. He doesn't know he's born yet!' And so the cleverness and the cynicism come in.

What is happening? It is sin robbing men and women of their most priceless possessions and reducing them, in the end, to nothing but cynicism and worldly wisdom and utter despair and hopelessness. And, as we saw earlier, it could all be illustrated even in terms of the physical body. Take that bright young fellow with his drink. Think of his liver and the diseased process that goes on in it. He is not aware of anything. Probably he will know nothing until the disease is too advanced for anything to be done. But it is there. Sin always takes something out of you. It is always robbing you: robbing you of nervous energy, robbing you of purity, robbing you of physical stamina, robbing you of all your uplifting idealistic hopes, and reducing you to a mere mass of cynicism, disease and decay.

But we must go further. Sin is also always a slavery – 'Your land, strangers devour it in your presence, and it is desolate, as overthrown by strangers.' Isaiah says: Here you are, in your own country still, but instead of being the bosses you are the slaves. The others have come in, and conquered you, and you have got to do what you are told. It is your own country, but while you are looking on, they

are eating up the fat of the land and leaving the mere
refuse to you.

That is a graphic description of slavery, and it is, of
course, the truth about the life of sin. You are mastered
by an alien power; you are mastered by strangers, by your
enemies – the devil, the world and the flesh, and all the
principalities and powers of evil. This is something we
touched on earlier. Sin is nothing but slavery and that is
the tragedy of men and women today who are not Christians. They are slaves to desires; slaves to lusts; slaves to
drink; slaves to gambling; slaves to 'the thing to do';
slaves to the social round. The poor pathetic slaves! They
think their life is marvellous, that it is freedom. They
regard religion as slavery while they are absolutely held in
and shut down by their circumstances and all these forces
within.

But not only that, they are utterly helpless. They cannot do anything about it. If they could, they would. Some
of them, poor things, finally get so desperate that they
commit suicide in their attempt to get free. They do not
do that suddenly, they have been struggling for years.
They want to get out of it all and they cannot. Some
emigrate, some resign from great posts and go off into the
country somewhere, all because of the slavery which
holds them helpless.

Even further, men and women in sin are filled with
shame. Did you notice this terrible phrase – what a
pregnant phrase it is – 'Your land, strangers devour it in
your presence'? That is what makes the devastation so
terrible. If they carted you away and then destroyed your
land when you were not there, it would not be quite so
bad, though it would be humiliating, even then. But this is
still worse: 'strangers devour it in your presence'. And
that is a terrifying picture of people held by sin. They look
on at themselves, as it were, and say to themselves, 'Is it
conceivable that I am still the same person I once was? I
remember a time when I wasn't like this. I had hopes. I

had desires which were beautiful. I was optimistic. I believed that something could be done. I hadn't lost my character, my purity. I hadn't lost my honour. I hadn't broken my word. Where is the person I once was? Strangers devoured it while I was looking on.' They look in the mirror and see the degeneration, the shame that accompanies it all.

Our Lord summed this up in a terrifying phrase. He said, 'When a strong man armed [the devil] keepeth his palace, his goods are in peace' (*Luke* 11:21). A man in sin is like the heir of a great estate who has been conquered and has to work like a slave on his own estate. This world was made for us and we were put into it as the lords of creation. We were meant to enjoy it, to be happy in it and to have a full life in it. But here we are on our own estate, and the strangers – the world, the flesh, the devil – are commanding us and dragooning us and we, in shame, look on at our own misery, too helpless to do anything about it. That is what sin does.

There is one further word. It is the last word in these two verses. 'The daughter of Zion is left as a cottage in a vineyard, as a lodge in a garden of cucumbers.' Oh, what a tragedy! Do you know the final truth about sin? It is a truth that to me is the most awful thing, the ultimate desolation. It is that sin, having taken all out of me, having fooled me and robbed me and turned me into a miserable, helpless slave, leaves me at the end as a lonely, isolated, miserable wreck! 'The heart,' says an Old Testament verse, 'knoweth his own bitterness' (*Pro.* 14:10).

There it is again in the story of the prodigal son. A famine arose in that land and all the son's friends left him. They were there while he still had some money, but the moment his pockets were empty, they all vanished. In real need now, he had to take a job with some great man in the country who kept a herd of swine. He took a job feeding the swine, and, poor fellow, he who had known such a

[81]

wonderful home, had to fill his belly with the husks that were given to the swine. There is an ominous note in the next phrase: 'and no man gave unto him'. The man who had given so much to other people, thinking they were his friends, who had squandered his goods in riotous living, always ready to pay for every round when he had pockets full of money – it was a good home he had come from and he had taken his share of the inheritance – had no friends in the hour of his need. He was like that empty cottage in a vineyard, that deserted lodge in a garden of cucumbers, utterly isolated and forsaken and forlorn.

But there is a character in the New Testament who gives us a still more awful and terrifying picture of this truth. This literally happened – this is not a parable. I am referring to Judas Iscariot who betrayed our Lord. It was greed that made him do it; it was lust for money. He had gone to the authorities, and they had said in effect: 'Well now, if you do this, it will be wonderful. We'll never forget you. If you really do this for us, you'll be our friend for ever.' So he decided to proceed with the betrayal.

They were all together, having that last supper, and our Lord said, 'I say unto you, that one of you shall betray me . . . He it is to whom I shall give a sop, when I have dipped it' (*John* 13:21, 26). Then he passed the piece of bread to Judas Iscariot, and we are told that after Judas had taken it, he rose up and went out, 'and it was night'. And it is always into the night that a man goes when he betrays his God and his Lord. But then this is what happened later on:

Then Judas, which had betrayed him, when he saw that he [Christ] was condemned, repented himself and brought again the thirty pieces of silver to the chief priests and elders, saying, I have sinned in that I have betrayed the innocent blood. And they said, What is that to us? see thou to that. And he cast down the pieces of silver in the temple, and departed,

[82]

The Desolation of Sin

and went and hanged himself.
(*Matt.* 27:3–5)

The poor man came to his senses. He realized what he had done and was unhappy. He went to the chief priests and elders and said: What can I do? I've betrayed innocent blood. I don't want your money, it's burning in my pockets, take it back. I'm unhappy. What can I do?

And they said: That's your business, not ours.

They left him to himself, isolated – yes, like the lodge in the garden of cucumbers, like this bit of a house there in the vineyard. Like the prodigal son, 'No man gave unto him.'

'See thou to that'!

And sin and its boon companions always do that with us. They leave us to ourselves when they have robbed us, and exhausted us. They leave us as helpless hulks and tell us to get on with it as best we can.

Is there anything more awful, more terrible, than the death of ungodly people? They have to leave their family, and their friends – they cannot take them with them, it is impossible. They have to leave their money, their profession, their business. They have to leave everything: 'Naked came I out of my mother's womb, and naked shall I return thither' (*Job* 1:21).

Where are they going? Well, they are going to pass through death; they are going out of the world into the land beyond; from time to eternity. They are making the most vital journey anyone can ever make. And where are they going? They do not know. They look into the eyes of their loved ones, but they do not know either because they have lived the same sort of life. They look for their friends, but they are not there. They are not interested any longer. There is a great dinner, a marvellous dance; a new drinking place is opening up! No, they are alone. They are going out alone, empty-handed, as deserted as a

[83]

lodge in a garden of cucumbers, with everybody looking
on and saying: 'See thou to that.' Don't cry and whimper,
don't ask us. That's your business, not ours.

No angels meet them. No one guides them. No one
welcomes them.

Am I drawing on my imagination? My answer is this:
one of the greatest philosophers that Germany has ever
produced, if not the greatest, and certainly their greatest
poet, was a man called Goethe. Goethe was not a Christian, and he did not believe this Christian teaching. He had
a great brain. He had read the classics. He knew the
philosophers. He was a great thinker, and he thought this
was all that was necessary. But there he was, lying on his
deathbed. Do you know what his last words were? They
were these: 'More light.' He was crying for more light.
Why? Oh, because he was in an impenetrable darkness,
and his great brain, and learning, and knowledge, and all
his great friends could not help him. The darkness
deepened and 'no man gave unto him'. All he could do
was cry out, 'More light.' He did not know the only One
who could give him that light. He could not sing that
great hymn:

> Abide with me! fast falls the eventide;
> The darkness deepens: Lord, with me abide!
> When other helpers fail, and comforts flee,
> Help of the helpless, O abide with me.
>
> Hold Thou Thy cross before my closing eyes,
> Shine through the gloom, and point me to the skies;
> Heaven's morning breaks, and earth's vain shadows
> flee;
> In life, in death, O Lord, abide with me.
> Henry Francis Lyte

Are you ready for that last journey? Will you have

someone to call on and to cry to who you know will answer you at that awful moment? There is only One who can do it. He is this blessed Son, whom God sent into the world to take away our guilt, to die in our stead, to bear our punishment and to reconcile us to God. He who has gone on before us says to all who believe in him, 'Let not your heart be troubled: ye believe in God, believe also in me. In my Father's house are many mansions: if it were not so, I would have told you. I go to prepare a place for you. And if I go and prepare a place for you, I will come again, and receive you unto myself; that where I am, there ye may be also' (*John* 14:1–3).

The contrast between sin and the gospel is that sin fools us, robs us, leaves us helpless, leaves us hopeless, leaves us desolate, whereas the gospel gives, and gives gloriously, gives continuously, gives endlessly. And the One who gives is the greatest gift of all, and he will never leave us nor forsake us if we believe in him.

6: *A Glimpse of Hope*

*

*Except the Lord of hosts had left unto us a very small remnant,
we should have been as Sodom, and we should have been like
unto Gomorrah.*   Isaiah 1:9

Isaiah has shown that sin leads to a life of misery and of
slavery and that ultimately it leaves us utterly helpless
and alone. But, thank God, the prophet has not finished.
We come now to this ninth verse which is the crucial verse
in this chapter because it is a kind of turning point in the
prophet's message. So far he has been depicting and
delineating sin: its nature, its character and its results.
And it is a most terrible picture. We must understand it;
we must believe it and accept it. But, thank God, the
prophet has another side to his message, and here in this
ninth verse we are at the point of transition. The verse is
a turning point because in it we are given a glimpse of
hope.

What a wonderful word is this word 'except'! It introduces the whole of the gospel, and that is what I want to
try to show you now. I put it to you that in this one verse
we have a perfect synopsis of the Christian message
which is something that the Bible is very fond of doing. It
likes to give us the message in a summary form like this,
so that we can remember it. Take, for example, John
3:16: 'For God so loved the world, that he gave his only
begotten Son, that whosoever believeth in him should not
perish, but have everlasting life.' There is the gospel in a
nutshell. And it is exactly the same here. I will summarize
the statement of the gospel in this verse under three
headings.

First, sin merits and deserves the punishment of total

destruction: 'Except [unless] the Lord of hosts had left unto us a very small remnant, we should have been as Sodom, and we should have been like unto Gomorrah.' What happened to them? Sodom and Gomorrah, the cities of the plain, were completely destroyed. There is a passage in Genesis where Abraham, looking down from the mountain tops where he had been living, saw in the distance those marvellous cities, which had been so flourishing, so full of happiness and enjoyment, and people having a good time, and suddenly they disappeared! 'Lo, the smoke of the country went up as the smoke of a furnace' (*Gen.* 19:28). Total destruction! And the prophet says here that as far as we are concerned that is precisely what we deserve.

The principle I am drawing from this is that, according to the teaching of the Bible, this is the truth about every single one of us. God sent his angels to destroy the cities of the plain as a punishment for their sin. Lot had been trying to plead with these people, and to tell them to stop their wicked ways, but they would not listen to him. And then at last God said: I shall destroy these cities because of their sin, their evil and iniquity.

And as we have seen, the prophet Isaiah says here to his fellow countrymen: If we had our deserts, that is what we would get – total destruction, with nothing left.

This is a very important point. Isaiah is saying that there is no plea that can be offered. Nothing can be said in mitigation of the sentence and of the wrath of God – nothing. And I want to emphasize this: it is always the first great statement of the Christian gospel. Before our Lord came, John the Baptist appeared. What was it he preached? He preached, 'the baptism of repentance for the remission of sins' (*Mark* 1:4). Here was the forerunner; here was the preparation for the gospel. Or, if you like, the law comes first, then the gospel. For, 'The law was given by Moses, but grace and truth came by Jesus Christ' (*John* 1:17). Repentance and belief in the

Lord Jesus Christ – that is the order.

Here, then, is the first step. We must realize that as members of the human race we deserve nothing but total destruction. Do we admit that? I am entitled to ask that question because I hear many people saying, 'Why does God not do something about it? Why does God not stop war? Why does he not put an end to this, that or the other?' They blame God for the condition of the world. But my message is that as long as men and women speak like that, there is no hope whatsoever. The first step is to do what Isaiah does here on behalf of the children of Israel, namely, to admit that they do not have a single plea, that they cannot ask for any mitigation, to confess that if they were to get their deserts, it would be total destruction.

But on what grounds do I say this? Let me give them to you. Why is it that men and women do not deserve any forgiveness at all? Well, look at man and woman as they were at the beginning. I put it to you. I turn you into members of the jury. What defence is there for Adam and Eve, made in the image of God, in Paradise, in absolute perfection with the friendship and the companionship of God, with all the blessings that anybody could ever desire? What did they do? They deliberately rebelled against God; they disobeyed him and put their own wills before his. Is there any excuse for them? Can any plea be put forward?

You might plead that they did it in ignorance. But they did not – they had been told; they had been warned. Nothing can be said for them. They had no defence and deserved not only to be driven out of Paradise, but to be destroyed totally and eternally.

But what about men and women ever since? Well, is it not exactly the same? What can be said on behalf of humanity? What plea can we enter in some kind of mitigation of the sentence of God upon sin? We cannot plead ignorance. Nobody will be able to say, 'But I didn't know.' God has made it quite plain and clear to us in the Bible what he expects of us, what he demands of us, and the kind of life that he would have us live. There are the Ten Commandments. They have been known throughout the running centuries.

But even if God had not given the law to Moses his servant, we all have a conscience, and our conscience renders us without any excuse at all. There is in every one of us a sense of right and wrong, of good and evil, and we must all confess that though we have known things to be wrong, we have still done them, and though we have known things to be right, we have not done them. 'For the good that I would, I do not: but the evil which I would not, that I do' (*Rom.* 7:19). We have deliberately flouted the voice of conscience. We have gone against this inward monitor that has warned us and condemned us beforehand. There is no excuse.

Not only that, we have history speaking to us. We have the history that is in the Bible, and also secular history confirms it. We have read what happens to people and to nations that disobey God. It is all here before us. We see what happened even to God's own people, the children of Israel, though they were as the apple of his eye. When they disobeyed him, they were carried away into captivity and their city was destroyed. It is all here before us. We see it in the case of great men: they have sinned and have suffered. It is there in the biographies; it is everywhere. The experience of the human race tells us that the life of sin is a life of folly; a suicidal life, a life that leads to misery and penury, and hopelessness at the end. We know it all, and yet, in spite of the knowledge we still persist in it.

But over and above all this, there is the gracious offer of the Christian gospel. Though we have gone astray and have brought our troubles upon ourselves, God has spoken and has said: Even though you have done this, I will receive you back. I will forgive you. I will give you a new start. I will send my Son to save you.

The offer of the gospel is before us. Yet the world rejects it. Our Lord himself has put that point in these words: 'And this is the condemnation, that light is come into the world, and men loved darkness rather than light, because their deeds were evil' (*John* 3:19). Now here is the evidence. The gospel is facing us, the light has come, but in spite of that, what is the attitude of men and women to God himself? It is arrogant and critical; it is contemptuous.

'If there is a God,' says the modern person, 'why doesn't he stop war? Why isn't he doing this and that?' Men and women stand up and criticize God, and in arrogance they venture to put their opinions before him. Is that not true? In spite of all that we have been considering, they not only deliberately disobey God, but do so boastfully, thinking they are clever. And not only that, they defy God. They stand up to him and say, 'Let God do his worst!' They are not afraid; they are in control! And on top of it all, as I have reminded you, they reject God's gracious offer in the gospel of his dear Son.

So what can be said? I repeat: What defence do you put up for the human race? What can you say in mitigation of God's sentence upon sin? What can you say to stop God punishing men and women as they deserve with 'everlasting destruction from the presence of the Lord' (*2 Thess.* 1:9)? What grounds of complaint would there be if God destroyed the whole human race as he destroyed Sodom and Gomorrah?

Here, then, is the first message of the gospel. We must see that, and we must confess it. 'Except the Lord of hosts had left unto us a very small remnant' that is what would have happened to us and we would have been unable to open our mouths because we have been fools. 'We are a sinful nation, a people laden with iniquity, a seed of evildoers, children that are corrupters,' says Isaiah. If God had blotted us all out for ever, we would not have a word of complaint to utter against him. Isaiah admits it for the nation; he admits it for himself. In the sixth chapter this is what I hear him saying, 'Woe is me! for I am undone; because I am a man of unclean lips, and I dwell in the midst of a people of unclean lips: for mine eyes have seen the King, the Lord of hosts' (*Isa.* 6:5).

And every other saint of God in the Bible does exactly the same thing. Look at David in Psalm 51: 'Against thee, thee only, have I sinned, and done this evil in thy sight' (verse 4). He is not defending himself. He is crying for mercy, for compassion. David does not get up and say, 'Oh God, I was greatly tempted and after all, I was only doing something very human. Why shouldn't I do this? Don't be hard on me. Why are you criticizing me?' No, David says, 'Have mercy upon me, O God.'

And that is the attitude of the tax collector whom our Lord commends in his parable of the tax collector and the Pharisee. The Pharisee is proud, justifying himself and boasting of his good works; the poor tax collector cannot even look up, he can just cry, 'God, be merciful to me a sinner' (*Luke* 18:13). That is the man, says our Lord, who went down to his house justified and blessed, the man who admits that he has no claim, that he is altogether sinful and that he has no plea and no excuse, but falls at the feet of God and cries out for mercy and compassion.

I must emphasize this point because it is the essential preliminary to the gospel. If you want to know the blessings of God, the blessings of the Lord Jesus Christ, and the blessings of the Christian gospel, the first thing you must do is admit that you have no claim at all upon them, that you do not deserve them, that actually you deserve nothing but punishment and hell. If you are still trying to defend yourself, if you still feel that God has not been fair to you, that God is unkind to you or that God has kept something back from you, you are not a Christian; you are still in the position of rebellious Adam and Eve; you are in the position of the Pharisees. Those who receive salvation and who get to know God and his blessings are those who confess, 'I admit the charge. I have been a fool. I have been a rebel. I have been vile and foul. If God were to blot me out and to throw me into hell, he would be doing what is absolutely right, and I would have no grounds of complaint.'

You will never know the blessings of salvation until you have cast yourself, just as you are, in utter helplessness upon the sole mercy of God. Sodom and Gomorrah are in us, every one – the lust, the evil, the foulness, not in the same form perhaps, although there is a great deal of that in our modern cities. This evil, this rebellion against God, this life of violence, this life of antagonism, this life of spitting upon God's law, it is in us all by nature. Are you ready to confess that God has a perfect right to cast you into everlasting destruction, out of his presence, and that if he behaved only in terms of justice and righteousness and law, that is what would happen?

That, then, is the first point that the prophet makes. The second point is that men and women are totally incapable of doing anything at all about their own salvation.

'Where do you find that?' asks someone.

Here it is: 'Except' – were it not for – 'Except the Lord of hosts had left unto us a very small remnant, we should have been as Sodom, and we should have been like unto Gomorrah.' Do you see what Isaiah is saying? He is saying that if God had not done something, the result would be destruction – which means that we can do nothing. Now here again is a most important point in connection with the gospel. People are never saved until they realize that they cannot save themselves. There is nothing that puts us further away from salvation than to think that we can save ourselves. Isaiah is saying here that men and women are completely incapable, so what is it that they cannot do?

First, they cannot evade God. Had you ever realized

that? Here is Israel in trouble, trying to get away from God, turning her back upon him, listening to other gods and to the false prophets. Yes, exactly like Sodom and Gomorrah! And poor Lot chose to live among them! He should not have done so. Abraham was wise and lived on the mountain tops, but Lot wanted to go to the cities of the plain, the fruitful land! That is what people are always doing. In their cleverness they think that they can get away from God. But that is an utter impossibility!

And that is the great message that is conveyed to us through the story of the children of Israel. All along they were trying to get away from God. They took up with the gods of the other nations, and they said, 'It's going to be all right, we've finished with God. Our God is too narrow – the Ten Commandments, and so on! *This* is the big life and the great life!' But they could not get away from him. Wherever they went, there he was, because he is everywhere. And this is the great lesson that the human race must learn. It does not matter where I am, says the psalmist in Psalm 139, God is always there.

> *Whither shall I go from thy spirit? or whither shall I flee from thy presence? If I ascend up into heaven, thou art there: if I make my bed in hell, behold, thou art there. If I take the wings of the morning, and dwell in the uttermost parts of the sea; even there shall thy hand lead me, and thy right hand shall hold me. If I say, Surely the darkness shall cover me; even the night shall be light about me. Yea, the darkness hideth not from thee; but the night shineth as the day: the darkness and the light are both alike to thee. For thou hast possessed my reins: thou hast covered me in my mother's womb.*
>
> (*Psa.* 139:7–13

And that is always true.

People think that if they can only get away from God they will find happiness, but they cannot. God is 'the hound of heaven' – 'I fled Him down the nights and down the days,' says Francis Thompson. People have been trying to get away from God throughout the centuries. During the last hundred years or so they have been saying, 'There is no God, and we don't need God. We're educated now! We've got science and we're going to make a perfect world for ourselves!' They thought they had finished with God, but they had not. God comes in and upsets their arrangements! Two world wars; things going wrong! Who is that? That is God. That is God punishing as he punished Sodom and Gomorrah, and more will come unless we repent and return to him. You cannot evade God; you cannot evade the punishment of God! It is foolish to try because you are getting old and you have to die, and there God meets with you and you cannot run away. You have not got the strength; your soul is ebbing out; life is going and there you are, face to face with God. How helpless we are.

But look at the other side. Not only can you not evade God, you can do absolutely nothing at all about putting yourself right with him. You may say to yourself, 'All right, I see I cannot run away from God. You're right. I've got to die and stand before God in the judgment. So I'm now going to start putting myself right with God!' But how are you going to do it? I will tell you the things which will prove to you that you can do nothing.

You cannot even create within yourself the desire for God. 'The carnal [natural] mind is enmity against God: for it is not subject to the law of God, neither indeed can be' (*Rom.* 8:7). Before you and I can make ourselves desire God, we must change our natures, we must change our hearts, and we cannot. The natural mind hates God and it can do nothing about making itself desire God.

But wait: can people *find* God? They may be convinced by this argument and they may say: 'All right, I accept the

[94]

fact that there is a God, and I shall now find him!' And they begin searching for God. But they cannot find him. Here is Job, a man at the dawn of history about whom we read in the Bible, and the book of Job expresses the question once and for ever: 'Canst thou by searching find out God?'

You cannot.

'Oh that I knew where I might find him!' says Job (*Job* 23:3). If only I could find him and state my case. But he could not. The apostle Paul came centuries later and said the same thing: 'The world by wisdom knew not God' (*1 Cor.* 1:21). The Greek philosophers were trying to find him and they could not. They knew there was another God; they called him 'the Unknown God'. They built an altar for him, but they could not find him. 'The Unknown God', where is he? He is so high; he is so great; he is so holy. 'The world by wisdom knew not God.' Men and women cannot find God even when they begin to search for him. But more, even if men and women could find God, what could they do about their past sins? What could they do about their crimes against God? They are totally helpless.

> *Not the labours of my hands*
> *Can fulfil Thy law's demands.*
> *Could my zeal no respite know,*
> *Could my tears for ever flow,*
> *All for sin could not atone;*
> *Thou must save, and Thou alone.*
>
> *Nothing in my hand I bring;*
> *Simply to thy Cross I cling.*
> Augustus Toplady

I can weep for the rest of my life, I can live in sackcloth and ashes, but I cannot make atonement.

Not only that, I cannot produce a righteousness for myself adequate to let me stand in the presence of God. 'Who shall ascend into the hill of the Lord?' (*Psa.* 24:3). Who shall dwell with that burning fire?

> *Eternal Light! Eternal Light!*
>   *How pure the soul must be,*
> *When placed within Thy searching sight,*
> *It shrinks not, but with calm delight,*
>   *Can live, and look on Thee!*

Who can do it?

> *O how shall I, whose native sphere*
>   *Is dark, whose mind is dim,*
> *Before the Ineffable appear,*
> *And on my naked spirit bear*
>   *The uncreated beam?*
>
> Thomas Binney

'God is light and in him is no darkness at all' (*1 John* 1:5). He sees every spot and stain. How can I cleanse my hands? Where can I find a robe of righteousness? It is impossible. 'All have sinned and come short of the glory of God' (*Rom.* 3:23).

And on top of it all, as we have seen, I cannot deliver myself from sin's foul bondage. We have seen the slavery of humanity: slavery to lust and to passion, slavery to the devil, to the mind of the world. 'Strangers devour your land in your presence, and it is desolate, as overthrown by strangers,' and you are helpless. You cannot do anything; they are stronger. You cannot escape, no matter how hard you try.

There, then, is the human condition. People cannot do anything about their own salvation. No one can conquer the world and the flesh and the devil; no one can answer the law of God; no one can stand righteous before God.

'Oh,' you say, 'but I have always done a lot of good!'

But in the sight of God your good is nothing but filthy rags. That is not my term, it is the Bible's. 'All our righteousnesses are as filthy rags' (*Isa.* 64:6). I will go further. The apostle Paul calls it 'dung' – manure. 'But what things were gain to me, those I counted loss for Christ. Yea doubtless, and I count all things but loss . . . but dung' (*Phil.* 3:7–8). Do not talk about your goodness in the sight of God. Here is absolute perfection, here is holiness without a blemish, and anything that you can produce is vile and foul, it cannot stand. And so we see the utter helplessness and hopelessness of all human beings – 'Except the Lord of hosts had left unto us a very small remnant, we should have been as Sodom, and we should have been like unto Gomorrah.'

And now, thank God for my last point. Our salvation is entirely of God – 'Except the Lord of hosts had left unto us a very small remnant' – but thank God he has. You know, says Isaiah to his fellow countrymen, were it not that God had left a remnant, we would all have been destroyed, every one of us, but he has left us a very small remnant! We could not do anything, we were completely helpless and deserved nothing but hell, but we are saved. It is he who has done it.

Here is the glory of the gospel and it is all pictured to us perfectly in that story of Sodom and Gomorrah. Lot and his family would have been destroyed were it not for the fact that God brought them out. The messengers, the angels of God, came to them and told them: Escape, escape for your life. God is going to destroy the cities. Get out – get out at once!

Then the Genesis account says, 'And while he lingered' (*Gen.* 19:16). Even though he had had the message, Lot lingered, as did his wife and daughters. So the angels came and put their hands upon the hands of Lot and his

family and led them out. They had to be led out forcibly
or they would have been entirely destroyed. Salvation is
entirely of God; it is his work from the beginning to the
very end.

And, you know, it is because of what God has done in
this way that I stand in this pulpit. What puts me here is
the word *except* – 'Except the Lord of hosts . . .' but he
has done it. I am here to announce: 'There is forgiveness
with thee, that thou mayest be feared' (*Psa.* 130:4). Look
at it: 'Except the Lord of hosts' had done it. He did it for
Israel and this is what he has done in his Son for the whole
human race. Look at the wonder of it! Have you ever
thought of the wonder of the fact that there is a gospel to
preach at all?

'Why do you say it is a wonderful thing?' asks someone.

I will tell you. God was under no obligation whatsoever to save us, as I have already demonstrated to you.
But he has done it! The God whom we have scorned and
offended, the God we have blasphemed, the God we have
disobeyed and criticized, is the very One who himself
delivers us. The One who has the power to consign us to
perdition, this Lord of hosts, uses that selfsame power in
our salvation and for our deliverance. Oh, what a
wonderful thing it is!

Our Lord once said to his fearful disciples, 'Be not
afraid of them that kill the body, and after that have no
more that they can do. But I will forewarn you whom ye
shall fear: Fear him, which after he hath killed hath
power to cast into hell' (*Luke* 12:4–5). That is the power
of God. He and he alone can cast into hell. But he uses
that very power to put us into heaven.

What is the explanation? Why has he done it? And the
answer is, because of his own character. Why is it that
God saves anybody at all? It is because he is God; it is
because he is a God of love and a God of grace, and of
mercy and of kindness and of compassion. It is because he

is a God who takes no delight in the death of the ungodly but rather that he should turn and be saved. What led God to make a way of salvation? Nothing but his own heart of love and of grace.

But then, look at the wisdom of God displayed in his planning and devising and preparing this wonderful way of salvation. And then, think of his power. Isaiah calls him 'the Lord of hosts', which means that he is the God who made the hosts of heaven, all the planets and the stars and the constellations. He controls them; they are all, as it were, at his fingertips. There is no end to his power, and that is the power he has used in our salvation.

Here and here alone is the power that can deliver us from the grip of the devil, from the grip of sin and lust and shame and evil, and even from hell itself. Here is a power that can create us anew, that can give us a new heart and mind, a new outlook and understanding, and a new hope and a fresh start – the power of God, the Lord of hosts. And here is the only power that is sufficient to help us and to lead us through the remainder of life, to take us through the last enemy, death itself, and finally into heaven and into everlasting glory! The hymnwriter has put it for us:

> *Stronger His love than death or hell;*
> *Its riches are unsearchable;*
> *   The first-born sons of light*
> *Desire in vain its depths to see;*
> *They cannot reach the mystery,*
> *   The length, and breadth, and height.*
>   Charles Wesley

I want to stop here with this thought, with the *fact* of it. 'Were it not that the Lord of hosts *had left* unto us . . .' This is not theory, this is not a fairy tale or a pious hope. 'Listen,' says Isaiah, in effect, 'He has done it. At this moment we would not have been here at all but would have been destroyed like Sodom and Gomorrah were it not that God had done this.' God would do it for the nation of Judah: they would be carried away to the captivity of Babylon, but he would bring a remnant back. Centuries earlier he had brought them out of Egypt. They were utterly helpless in Egypt; it was God who brought them out with that mighty hand of his that can divide a Red Sea, divide the river Jordan, take them through the wilderness and give them manna. Here is the power that saves.

And, I repeat again, I am a preacher because of what God has done. This is not a theory. I am here to present to you an historical gospel. I am here to tell you what God has actually done about you and about your salvation. He promised at the beginning that the seed of the woman would bruise the serpent's head (*Gen.* 3:15). Yes, says David, he has 'laid help upon one that is mighty' (*Psa.* 89:19). It needed someone stronger than Satan to deliver us and no human being could do that.

> *O loving wisdom of our God!*
> *When all was sin and shame,*
> *A second Adam to the fight*
> *And to the rescue came.*
> John Henry Newman

A second Adam – who is he? Christ, the Son of God, the babe of Bethlehem, the mighty One of God. Stronger than hell, stronger than the devil, stronger than evil, the mighty conqueror, the everlasting king, the One who carries the government upon his shoulders – he is the One whom God has sent. 'God so loved the world, that he gave [he has given] his only begotten Son, that whosoever believeth in him should not perish, but have everlasting life' (*John* 3:16).

A Glimpse of Hope

Why is it that the whole world is not in hell at this moment? Why is it that a remnant has been saved to dwell in the glory everlasting? There is only one reason – 'When the fulness of the time was come, God sent forth his Son, made of a woman, made under the law, to redeem them that were under the law' (*Gal.* 4:4–5).

Are you resting in this *except*? Are you holding on to it? Having seen your guilt and utter helplessness, do you know? Do you believe? Have you accepted the fact that God has sent his only Son into the world in order to bear your punishment on the cross and redeem you, in order to take hold of you and take you out of the kingdom of darkness and put you into the kingdom of his dear Son? Do you know it? Have you felt that power? 'I am not ashamed of the gospel of Christ,' wrote Paul to the Romans. Why? 'for it is the power of God unto salvation to every one that believeth' (*Rom.* 1:16).

This is not a message telling you to pull yourself together and haul yourself up by your boot laces. This is not telling you to turn over a new leaf and live a better life and use great will power and get people to help you and encourage you. It cannot be done. You are saved by the power of the Lord of hosts, the almighty and the everlasting God who, having made you at the beginning, can make you again. He can make a new man or woman of you and give you something of his own divine nature once more, and lead you until you are safely with him in the glory everlasting.

7: *Repentance*

*

Hear the word of the Lord, ye rulers of Sodom; give ear unto the law of our God, ye people of Gomorrah. Isaiah 1:10

The prophet here starts a new paragraph in this introduction to his great message which can be divided into two sections. The first is a description, a delineation, of the condition of the children of Israel; it is a diagnosis, an exposing of the causes of their trouble. The second section is the application of the remedy. That is a summary of the whole of the Bible. There are only two divisions in the Bible: the law and the gospel; Old Testament and New Testament. That is a rough but good classification. We must never lose sight of it; we must never get lost in all the details of the Bible. We must always keep our minds fixed upon these great central, pivotal principles. And we have been watching Isaiah as he does that.

In his first paragraph Isaiah gives us a description of sin, showing us its essence and its character, what it really is and how it comes about. Then he goes on in his second paragraph, starting at verse 5, to show us the consequences of sin and evil, and he paints these consequences in terrifying and almost lurid colours. And we come to the point, in the ninth verse, in which he shows the ultimate result of sin – 'Except the Lord of hosts had left unto us a very small remnant, we should have been as Sodom, and we should have been like unto Gomorrah.' It is as bad as that.

Now, therefore, the question arises: What next? And, thank God, the prophet goes on; he does not leave us merely in a state of utter condemnation and hopelessness.

[102]

He brings us there, but he does not leave us there. And it is at this point that the gospel pure and simple begins to speak. It is one of the points of transition from law to gospel. Of course, we have had hints of the gospel already. There were hints of the gospel even in the law given to Moses. There were burnt offerings and sacrifices, and that is gospel in the Old Testament, in the law. But though the grace and mercy of God are revealed even in the law, its main function is to bring us to conviction, to show us our need, to reveal our plight and show us our helplessness.

So we are at the point of transition, and I put it like that deliberately because it seems to me that we are at a very important juncture. 'What next?' I say. Yes, but the important question is: Have *you* said, 'What next?' Anyone who has followed the first nine verses and has understood their message, anyone who has seen its truth and believed it, is now desperately asking that question.

Let us look at that question in a New Testament form. In Acts 2 we are given an account of how the apostle Peter stood up and addressed the people who were at Jerusalem, both the citizens of Jerusalem and the Jews who had come up from all parts of the civilized world for the feast of Pentecost. We read that all the disciples had been together in the Upper Room when suddenly the Holy Spirit had come upon them, and the people outside had come crowding together asking, 'What meaneth this?' Then Peter, as the spokesman, began to speak to them, and what he did was to expound and to apply the Old Testament scriptures. He began to tell the crowds about the Lord Jesus Christ whom they had crucified, and he showed them how he was the One of whom the prophets had prophesied that his soul would not remain in hell or his body see corruption, but that he would rise from the dead.

Then notice what happened next. The preacher was suddenly interrupted by the congregation, and what did they say? They shouted out, 'Men and brethren, what shall we do?' They showed that they had seen that 'Except the Lord of hosts . . .' They saw what they were like and they said: What can we do? How can we get out of that? We don't want to have the fate of Sodom and Gomorrah!

If you prefer it in terms of an individual, take the story in Acts 16. Paul and Silas had been put in prison. Then, there was a great earthquake and the jailer, fearing that all the prisoners had fled, would have killed himself, but he was reassured by the voice of Paul saying to him, 'Do thyself no harm: for we are all here.' So the jailer came to them trembling, and as he looked at them and marked their composure in spite of the earthquake and everything else, the man said, 'Sirs, what must I do to be saved?' He said in effect, 'What must I do to be like you? I'm convicted; I can see that I'm all wrong. You have something that I haven't got! What is this? Tell me!' You see, he was under deep conviction and he wanted guidance, exactly like the people in Jerusalem at Pentecost.

And this is something that is an invariable rule when God brings men and women to deliverance and to a knowledge of salvation. They listen to the description of sin; they see it as rebellion against God, as perversion – 'The ox knoweth his owner, and the ass his master's crib . . .' And they begin to realize it is true of them. They have seen the nature of sin; they have seen themselves as rebels, as fools; and they have seen something of the consequences that follow. And when they have really seen it, their next question is: What now? What can I do? How can I get out of this position?

Have you felt that? Is that true of your experience? As we have seen, that is an important question. The world is not interested in Christ for the simple reason that it does not see any need of him. Campaigns are held and evangelists shout: 'Come to Christ.' But the people do not come to Christ, the masses do not come to him, because they see no relevance in all this. Why should they come to Christ? They are all right as they are, they say. In fact, it has never been so good!

No, you must have a reason for coming – 'They that are whole have no need of the physician, but they that are sick: I came,' says Christ, 'not to call the righteous, but sinners to repentance' (*Mark* 2:17). The Pharisees never believed in him, they rejected him; it was the tax collectors and the harlots who went crowding into the kingdom. Why? Because they had seen their need of him. They were the people who were crying out in different ways, 'What shall I do?'

Now all that is involved between verses 9 and 10 because the prophet goes on to say this: 'Hear the word of the Lord, you rulers of Sodom; give ear unto the law of our God, you people of Gomorrah.' If you do not want to be overwhelmed, as the cities of the plain were, listen. If you are asking what must be done, here is the answer: 'Listen.'

Verse 10 is what we may very well describe as *the call to repentance* and this is a most important matter. I have already reminded you of how the people cried out as they interrupted Peter's sermon on the day of Pentecost – 'Men and brethren, what shall we do?'

Back came the answer: 'Repent, and be baptized every one of you in the name of Jesus Christ for the remission of sins, and ye shall receive the gift of the Holy Ghost' (*Acts* 2:38). That is the answer: 'Repent and believe.' But repent first, then go on to your belief. The Bible indicates to us that this is always the way when people reach the point when they cry, 'What shall I do?'

It is easily demonstrable that repentance must always come first – and that is always the way to Christ and salvation. The first preacher in the New Testament is John the Baptist and he preached 'the baptism of repentance for the remission of sins' (*Luke* 3:3). He was the forerunner, the voice crying in the wilderness, 'Prepare ye the way of the Lord.' The apostle Paul reminded the elders of the church at Ephesus that day and night, both in public and in private and with tears, he had preached, 'repentance toward God and faith toward our Lord Jesus Christ' (*Acts* 20:21).

So the first message of the gospel is not, 'Come to Jesus,' it is, 'Repent.' I will go further and say that no one truly comes to Jesus without repentance – it is impossible. There is no such thing as a Christian who has never repented. The Holy Spirit is a Spirit of light, and a Spirit of order and of method. He always does these things in the same way, as God does in all creation, in everything. In this great matter of salvation, he does God's work on a system and on a principle.

These are vital matters. We cannot afford to play with these things, life is too urgent, too desperate. You see, you can think you are a Christian, and not be a Christian. You can have a nice feeling and think that means, 'I am a Christian.' But it does not necessarily follow. Do you know why you are a Christian? Do you know what it means to be a Christian? Can you 'give an answer to every man that asketh you a reason of the hope that is in you' (*1 Pet.* 3:15)? Now that is where repentance comes in. The true Christian has first repented and then believed. And I cannot think of a better way of putting the doctrine of repentance than this verse that we are now considering: 'Hear the word of the Lord . . . give ear unto the law of our God.'

'What must I do?' says someone.

Let us divide it up like this. The English word 'repent' comes from a Latin word which means to think again. To think again is always the first step. Look at it in terms of these children of Israel. They had been turning their backs upon God; they had all gone their own way; they were 'laden with iniquity, a seed of evildoers, children that are corrupters'. They 'provoked the Holy One of Israel unto anger, they are gone away backward' (*Isa.*

[106]

1:4). Because of these things, God had been punishing them but, as we have seen, they went on with their sinful life. 'Why should ye be stricken any more? Ye will revolt more and more' (verse 5). They were covered with bruises and open sores and yet they went on in this wrong way saying: I shall continue. I'm not going to listen.

So Isaiah is saying: In the name of God, stop for a moment and ask questions.

Let me give you the great New Testament illustration of all this. The prodigal son leaves home and, with his pockets full of money, goes to a far country where he has a wonderfully good time! But famine comes and the money all goes. Yet he still does not think at all. The devil does not allow us to think; he just keeps us going on and on. If only we stopped and did some thinking, we would soon leave him, but he does not allow us to do that. And there is that poor fellow there in the field with the swine and the husks. What is the turning point in his story? 'He came to himself and he said . . .' (*Luke* 15:17). What does he say? It is something like this: 'What in the name of conscience am I doing in a place like this? What is my father's son doing in a field sitting down among swine and eating husks? What does it mean? What's happened to me? Where is my brain, my reason? What sort of fool am I?'

He begins to talk to himself – he begins to think – and it is only then that he really does begin to think. Before that he has only grumbled, and while you are grumbling you are not thinking, you are just complaining because the money is going and because the famine has come. Thinking means that you face the situation. So the prodigal son begins to do that, and it is the means of his eventually going home.

So, then, says the Bible, if you have recognized the cause of your trouble, and seen that the things that are happening to you are the consequences of what you have been doing, and of your rebellion against God, stop and think. Pull yourself up. Say, 'Now I am going to face things.' If you do, you begin to ask yourself questions: Where am I going? How have I arrived in this position? Why are certain things true of me now that used not to be true of me? What has brought it about? Why have I done it? What advantages have I derived?

Then you ask: Where am I going? What is the meaning of life? What is the meaning of humanity? What am I doing in this world? Do I just go on round and round in a never-ending circle? What is it going to lead to? What is the ultimate end of all this? Where am I going to find myself? Furthermore, what about death? What lies beyond? I've just gone on doing the things that I've been wanting to do, and see everybody else doing. Nobody has stopped to think or to ask questions. I see now that I've got to stop.

Of course, you may say that you *have* already thought and that the life you have been living is the result of it. All right! Those were your modes of thought; that was your philosophy of life. But now you realize that you are in trouble. So what do you do? You think again – that is all. You examine your philosophy. You say, 'Now I really am going to look at this seriously and soberly. I shall not continue to go round and round in circles. Like the prodigal son, you 'come to yourself'.

That, then, is the first step in repentance. And, of course, I take it that you are clear about this. When I say that we must think, I do not mean that we go on repeating the clichés. That is not thinking, it is a substitute for thought. I must not go on about this now, but I think that we all need to be taught how to think. I know many people today who do not think, they only read books! Ah, but you say that reading books makes you think. Are you sure? Are you sure that when you read a book you do not just repeat it like a parrot? Repeating things you have read is not thinking. A machine can do that, a parrot can do it! Thinking is a process in which you do not just repeat the clichés, and say what everybody else is saying.

No, you sit down and say, 'I wonder if all that is right? I know that it is what everybody says, but look what it leads to in the world. I must examine this.'

Have you really thought about life? I do not care what age you are. You may be young. Have you thought what the meaning of life is? Do you know where you are going? I ask the question still more to the middle-aged who have settled down in life, perhaps. I ask it to the aged: Have you thought? Think again – 'Hear the word of the Lord, ye rulers of Sodom; give ear unto the law of our God, ye people of Gomorrah.' If you do not, you will be involved in the disaster.

The second meaning of 'repent' is, 'change your mind'.That is the literal meaning of the Greek word for repentance – *metanoia*. The Latin, 'think again', and the Greek, 'change your mind' together give us a complete meaning. Repentance is not only thinking again, because if you do that it does not follow, of course, that you will come to the correct conclusion. You may arrive at the same thoughts as before, you may confirm yourself in your previous decision, and that is not repentance. Repentance involves a change of mind.

So when the prophet calls upon us to hear, he says: I want you to listen and to think in a particular way. Repentance involves a realization that we have been all wrong in our thinking. That is a terrible blow to us, is it not? Particularly today, when we are so proud of our thinking and our philosophy. The first thing the gospel asks us to do is admit that we have been wrong in our thinking – and equally wrong, therefore, in our living and in our entire behaviour. That is what the Bible is saying to the whole world today, to the world in sin, in its shame, its sorrow, its anguish, where there is starvation in one country and plenty in another. Some people are dying because they do not have enough, while others are throwing food into the sea, or burning it because it is surplus. That is the world, that is what men and women have

brought it to. People in their cleverness! It is not God who
has done that, it is men and women departing from God
who have done it. There was no problem like that in
Paradise; that is humanity's work.

Let me sum this up by giving you the classic example of
it – none other than the apostle Paul. There he was, that
proud, self-righteous Pharisee, hating Jesus Christ,
blaspheming his name and trying to exterminate the
Christian Church. Why did he do it? Well, as he told
Agrippa and Festus when he was on trial – and what a
confession it was – 'I verily thought with myself . . .'
Exactly! 'I verily thought with myself, that I ought to do
many things contrary to the name of Jesus of Nazareth'
(*Acts* 26:9). *He* was everything, speaker and audience,
talking to himself and agreeing with himself! And that is
what we all do until we become Christians. We defend
ourselves and put up a case that we can answer. We are
marvellous at this: we talk to ourselves and we think with
ourselves, and we know we are right: we are unanimous!

But when the Spirit of God takes hold of the word of
God and speaks to us, we cease to be unanimous and
realize that we have been totally wrong. 'I did it in
ignorance, in unbelief,' said Paul in effect. 'I thought I
knew so much, but I was a fool, I knew nothing!' We
admit that all our thinking and all our living have been
altogether wrong and confess it to God, without making
any excuses.

Paul wrote to the church in Corinth, God has 'made
foolish the wisdom of this world' (*1 Cor.* 1:20) and no
one is a Christian until he sees that. Every one of us is
born with the mind and the outlook and the philosophy
of the world. 'The world was very old indeed when you
and I were young,' says E. C. Bentley. Exactly! We all are
born as old men and women; we have received the thinking and the philosophy of humanity in sin and we absorb
it almost with our food and with the very breath that we
breathe in. We have to be convinced that it is all wrong,

that the wisdom of this world is the cause of the mess that the world is in. We must confess this; it is an essential part of repentance.

We have not repented until we have done what David did in Psalm 51. He confesses, 'Against thee, thee only, have I sinned, and done this evil in thy sight' (verse 4). 'Have mercy upon me, O God' (verse 1). We must say, 'Whatever made me do it? What's wrong with my thinking that I should ever have done such a thing? I even wanted to do it, and justified myself in doing it! God, I have been all wrong. Cleanse me, give me a new mind. "Renew a right spirit within me"!' That is always the second step.

The third point is that in the light of this, men and women must cease, therefore, to rely any more upon their own capacity and their own wisdom: they must. The challenge that comes to them in 1 Corinthians 1:20 is this: 'Where is the wise? where is the scribe? where is the disputer of this world?' Those are the questions that the great apostle hurls at those clever Greeks in Corinth to whom he was writing. Have you heard those questions addressed to you? You are wise; you are a scribe; you are a reader; you are a student; you are a disputer. You are the clever one in the debating society. You can put the world right. You can always prove your argument and you get applause from all who are listening to you. Where are you, disputer of this world? What have you got to say? 'Hath not God made foolish the wisdom of this world?'

And if ever that was true of any generation, it is surely true of this one. Look what the wisdom of this world has brought us to. In the twentieth century, it has not been 'the thing to do' to believe in God. Indeed, 'the thing to do' has been *not* to believe in him – to ridicule Christianity, to say that it is sob stuff, opium of the people. The clever person, the disputer of this world, the wise, the scribe, the learned, sophisticated person, has ridiculed it all. But what has such wisdom produced? Where has it landed us? Where is it leading us? What has it to give us? Is it not about time that we began asking these questions? And I would hold that Christian men and women are people who admit that they no longer have confidence in their own minds nor in the minds of others. They are ready to admit that they are all inadequate.

Have you come to that or are you still holding on to the wisdom of this world? Do you really believe that the statesmen understand the cause of our ills? Do you believe that the philosophers understand it any better? The scribes, the disputers of this world, are patently failing; they are entirely at sea; they are absolutely baffled and bewildered. And so are you. Are you ready to admit that yet, or are you still putting your faith in your own brain, in your own reasoning power and in all the propositions that you can put up?

Now all this is implied here: 'Hear the word of the Lord,' which means that you no longer rely on your own word nor the word of anybody else; you have finished with the wisdom of the world. The extraordinary thing that sin does to us is that it makes us hold on to our opinions and our views, and though the world is on fire around and about us, we still think we can understand and deal with it! But if you really want to know what to do next, says the Bible, there is your answer: 'Hear the word of the Lord.'

I do not expect you to believe this gospel message if you believe some of the modern philosophers; it would be folly for me to expect it! If you are a logical positivist, if you are a follower of Bertrand Russell, you will not believe the word of God. If you put your faith in that philosophy, the Bible will be nonsense to you. You must finish with the one first and then, and only then, will you be ready to listen to the other. And if, after listening to the Bible's analysis of the nature of sin, and having looked at the consequences of sin in yourself, and in society and in the whole world, you can still go on putting your faith in that modern philosophy, then all I can say to you is that you are very much in Sodom and Gomorrah. And if you do not change your mind and if you do not give that up, then beyond any question you will be involved in a final destruction.

That, then, brings me to my last point, which is that the final step in repentance is utter submission to God's word – 'Hear the word of the Lord, ye rulers of Sodom; give ear unto the law of our God, ye people of Gomorrah.' Sit down, stop, give up, listen. That means – and this is absolutely vital – acceptance of revelation. Let me put it in the words that I am so fond of quoting. The great Blaise Pascal saw this fact very clearly. He was a brilliant mathematician, with a fine French mind; its logic and debating capacity have probably never been surpassed. And this is how Pascal put it: 'The supreme achievement of reason is to bring us to see that there is a limit to reason.' And the moment we see that there is a limit to reason, and not until then, we are ready to listen to revelation. And this is the very thing that is held before us here. You must submit utterly and entirely 'to the word of the Lord, and unto the law of our God'. What does that mean? It means that with regard to the great problems of humanity and life and living and death and eternity, with regard to the great problem of what makes the world what it is at the present time, and all the agony and the shame and the remorse and the suffering, with regard to all this, it means believing that the only wisdom that has an answer is the Bible.

What is the Bible? It is God's word, God's revelation. We must renounce human wisdom and say, 'I want the wisdom of God that I find here.' The Bible is not a collection of books in which men have expressed their own wisdom and thoughts. As we have seen, it was written by men who say that God came to them and spoke to them and opened their eyes and gave them a message. They

say: I don't do this of myself, the Spirit came upon me.
God gave me this burden. God gave me this message and
I just repeat it. It is not mine, it is his.

To submit to God's word, then, means that from our
hearts we believe and say that the Bible is God's revelation, and renouncing every other guidance and teaching
and wisdom and philosophy, we submit ourselves as little
children to the Bible. We believe that here we have the
mind of God. Here we have God speaking to us and
telling us about himself. Here we have God telling us that
he is over all and that he is the Creator, that there would
never have been a world at all if he had not made it. Here
we have God telling us the truth about humanity – that
man and woman were made in the image of God, and
made for God with glorious possibilities. Here we are
given God's wisdom with regard to what is the matter
with humanity and why the world is as it is.

And here, thank God, is the thing we want to know
most of all: how we can be delivered. Here is God's plan
and God's wisdom with respect to our salvation. The
apostle Paul says, 'We preach Christ crucified, unto the
Jews a stumblingblock, and unto the Greeks foolishness;
but unto them which are called, both Jews and Greeks,
Christ the power of God and the wisdom of God' (*1 Cor.*
1:23–24). This is it – we are hearing the word of the
Lord, and we are giving ear to the law of our God. In the
Bible we find a message that tells us that there is only one
way whereby we can be delivered: it is God's way and
here it is. This is God's wisdom.

And what is God's way? It is not that God has sent us
another teaching, a new philosophy, which we must
strive hopelessly to keep, but that 'God so loved the
world, that he sent his only begotten Son.' We find the
preparation for his coming in the Old Testament, and
then in the New Testament we find his coming, his teaching, his miracles, his death, his burial, his resurrection, his
sending of the Spirit, his sending out the apostles, and

[114]

their message concerning him. Here it is, this is God's way of salvation.

So that is what repentance means – that, having come to the end of our own wisdom, and of all other human wisdom, we submit ourselves utterly and absolutely to this message because it is the wisdom of God. To do this is not easy because our natural prejudices are against it – 'unto the Jews a stumblingblock, and unto the Greeks [nothing but, just] foolishness'. It is unlike anything we have ever heard.

'What!' asks somebody. 'Are you asking me just to believe that and then all will be well? It's not like that in the world! I've had to earn everything I've got. I had to work for my exams. I've had to work to make money in my business. And yet you say, "Take it all for nothing!" It's impossible, it's against everything I believe, everything I've experienced. It's against all my prejudices.'

All right, I agree. But if you are a Christian, in spite of everything, you will believe it. Why? Because here is something that starts with the supposition that we are all failures, and that is not what people say, but God. The gospel of Jesus Christ cuts across all our preconceived ideas. It tells us that we are all fools, that we are all muddled in our thinking, that we have all gone astray in our thinking. Who likes to be told that? But whether we like it or not, that is the message of the gospel – God has made this world's wisdom foolish and he has given us his own wisdom. 'Not many wise men after the flesh, not many mighty, not many noble, are called' (*1 Cor.* 1:26). Of course not! Why? Because they are proud of their intellects; they believe they understand. They are still holding on to their thoughts though their world is in chaos. Fools! Christians are people who have repented, who have thought again and seen that they cannot think aright. They say, 'Very well, I cannot help myself. I'm to come as a little child, as Christ told me to come.' He said, 'Except ye be converted, and become as little children, ye shall not enter into the kingdom of heaven' (*Matt.* 18:3). Little children do not understand, they believe. They take what is given to them. And you must be like that, says Christ. Come, follow me. Follow me in your mind. Follow me in everything. Confess you cannot do it. Just follow.

You must do that, in spite of your prejudices; you must do it, also, in spite of your failure to understand it fully. Oh, this is, again, very difficult, is it not? Men and women, with their pride of intellect, want to understand everything. They say, 'I'm not going to believe a thing if I don't understand it. You say I must believe in God, but I can't understand him.'

And because of that, they do not believe in God; they do not realize that they are making fools of themselves. If you could understand God, you would be equal to God! By definition, God cannot be understood. What you do in the presence of God is not try to understand, but bow down and worship – mystery!

Oh, yes, says Paul, we 'speak wisdom among them that are perfect: yet not the wisdom of this world, nor of the princes of this world, that come to nought: but we speak the wisdom of God in a mystery, even the hidden wisdom . . .' (*1 Cor.* 2:6–7). What is this? It is the mystery of God in Christ reconciling the world unto himself. You cannot understand the doctrine of the Trinity – three Persons and yet just one Godhead! You cannot understand the mystery of Christ. 'Great is the mystery of godliness: God was manifest in the flesh' (*1 Tim.* 3:16). There I look at him and see a man and yet he is God. He is divine and eternal and he is human within time. Can you understand that? Of course not! You try, but it seems utter folly.

You do not understand, but you believe because you see it before you. He has lived in history; you see what he has done. There he is. I do not understand him, I just fall at his feet in adoration, and I rise up and follow him. You believe in spite of your lack of understanding. If you wait until you understand, you will never believe. You must be

[116]

content not to understand. 'If any man among you seemeth to be wise in this world,' says Paul again to the Corinthians, 'let him become a fool, that he may be wise' (*1 Cor.* 3:18). Let him admit that he knows nothing, let him receive the revelation, then he will begin to understand and he will go on understanding, throughout the countless ages of eternity.

So you believe in spite of your prejudices, though you do not understand, and in spite of the laughter and derision of the world. The world will say that you have surrendered your intellect, while it is holding on to its intellect – the intellect that does not understand, that does not know what man is, or what life is, or why things are as they are and that cannot devise a way of salvation. All civilization has failed. All human efforts come to nought. And yet people pour scorn upon the Christian who says, 'I see now that I cannot understand and nobody else can. I will accept and believe and submit to the wisdom of God.'

Let the world laugh! Let the world go on laughing at Christianity; let it laugh itself into hell. Let it make its clever jokes. Let it get its applause – it will not last long. The actors and the clappers – they are all dying and will all go to destruction. The world laughed at the Son of God; it ridiculed him; it poured scorn upon him. 'Aha,' it said, 'he who saved others; let him save himself' (*Luke* 23:35). How clever! It laughed at him and did not realize that it was laughing at itself.

> *Let the world deride or pity,*
> *I will glory in Thy name.*
> John Newton

So if you want to know what to do, here is the only answer: 'Hear the word of the Lord . . . give ear unto the law of our God.' Everything you need is here. Whatever you may have done until this moment, I do hope that you are now ready to say like Samuel, 'Speak; for thy servant heareth' (1 Sam. 3:10). Or, say with Saul of Tarsus – who thought so much with himself and was so proud of his thinking yet fell to the ground on the road to Damascus – 'What wilt thou have me to do?' (Acts 9:6).

And here is the answer: 'Hear the word of the Lord . . .' Believe this message, accept the wisdom of God, and you will find yourself a new person in a new world with a new mind and above all a new hope and a new power. You will not only be enabled to live, you will be enabled to die, and you will know that beyond death you will go to be with Christ which is far better, to be with God, to be in the glory everlasting.

8: *God's Way Not Ours*

*

Hear the word of the Lord, ye rulers of Sodom; give ear unto the law of our God, ye people of Gomorrah. To what purpose is the multitude of your sacrifices unto me? saith the Lord: I am full of the burnt offerings of rams, and the fat of fed beasts; and I delight not in the blood of bullocks, or of lambs, or of he goats. When ye come to appear before me, who hath required this at your hand, to tread my courts? Bring no more vain oblations: incense is an abomination unto me; the new moons and sabbaths, the calling of assemblies, I cannot away with; it is iniquity, even the solemn meeting. Your new moons and your appointed feasts my soul hateth: they are a trouble unto me; I am weary to bear them. And when ye spread forth your hands, I will hide mine eyes from you: yea, when ye make many prayers, I will not hear: your hands are full of blood.

Isaiah 1:10–15

We have already considered the tenth verse which introduces the statement that is found in verses 11–15. And, of course, we have seen that it follows on from what the prophet has been saying in the first nine verses. It is very important that we should carry the whole message in our minds. There is a progression here. Prophets and biblical writers – prophets in the Old Testament and apostles in the New, writing their letters – did not just say the first thing that came to their minds. There is always an order in the thought, and a progress in the order; one thing leads to another. We are saved by believing the truth, not by having our feelings moved and disturbed without quite knowing what has been happening to us. No, to be saved is to 'come unto the knowledge of the truth' (*1 Tim.* 2:4).

As we have seen in the first nine verses, the prophet has been holding the people face to face with the nature and character and horror of sin. He has shown them what it leads to and, above everything else, he has shown them their precarious position as the result of their sinfulness. He has told them that not a single person would have been left were it not for the mercy and compassion, the love and grace of God.

Then, having brought them to a realization of their position, Isaiah begins to tell them about the only way of escape, the only solution, the only salvation. And we have seen that this message is contemporary, that it is speaking to us as much as it spoke to the people in Jerusalem in Isaiah's time. The word of God is one and it is always the same. There is no difference in humanity, sin is still sin, and there is no difference in God. The fact that all this was written eight centuries before Christ came, does not make the slightest difference. So we must listen to the word of God and submit to revelation. That is the first and essential step.

Now we have seen that quite clearly but it is not enough just to say that. The prophet goes on to add something to that, and we must follow him. Let me put it to you in the form of a principle: we must listen to all that God says. We must not listen to him in a piecemeal manner; we must not pick and choose. We must not come to the Bible and say: 'Ah, yes, I agree with this but I do not agree with that. I accept this; I reject that.' The moment we do that, we have gone from the first and essential foundational principle.

It is not enough to say that I am now prepared to be interested in God and to listen in general to the message of the Bible. I have, in particular, to submit to the Bible's teaching concerning the one and only way of salvation. And that is what is outlined for us in these verses that we are now considering. This is an extraordinary and a remarkable thing. 'Listen,' says the prophet, 'you must hear the word of the Lord, you must give ear to the law of our God.' The two things must be done – they are not the same. You must hear the word of the Lord in general;

then you come to the law and there you have the particulars. You must descend to details. It is all or nothing. You must take it as it is. Men and women have never been saved unless they have submitted absolutely to the gospel way of salvation.

That, then, is what the prophet puts before us, and you notice that he puts it in an extraordinary manner. Having described the condition, he says, 'Now hear the word of the Lord, give ear unto the law of our God.'

'Right,' we say, 'we're ready to listen.' And we expect some positive message but just when we think that Isaiah would have brought in his wonderful offer, this is what we get: 'To what purpose is the multitude of your sacrifices unto me?' Isaiah goes on until verse 15 with a purely negative word. God is telling them: What you are doing is no good. Stop doing it. I am not interested.

Negative! Surely this is an extraordinary thing, and there is only one explanation. Even when we have been awakened to the danger of our position and to a realization that there is something radically wrong with us, even when we are a bit alarmed about the state of our souls and our eternal destiny, even then, our instinct still is to do the wrong thing. That is why the gospel almost invariably starts with a negative. We have to be told not to do that, before we are told what to do.

Here, then, is a great message, here is a great principle that one finds everywhere in the Bible. Anybody who knows the long and chequered history of the children of Israel will know that failure to continue in God's way was always their particular trouble. What a life they lived! God spoke to them and blessed them, and they were as they should be for a while, but they would wander away from him, and things would begin to go wrong. Then they would say: 'What can we do?' And they would always do the wrong thing, and the prophets would be sent by God to tell them: Now that is wrong. You mustn't do that. That is not the way at all, this is the way.

And they would listen, and come back and be blessed again, only to repeat that backsliding all over again. And so this prophetical message is always a kind of repetition of itself. We see the classic example of that in the case of Saul, the first king of Israel. There was a man chosen of God and set up as king, and then he did the wrong thing and was dismissed and rejected. What was the matter with him? It was exactly what we have here.

When we come to the New Testament, we find this too. It is amazing to see the amount of time and space that is given to the recounting of the arguments and disputations between our Lord and Saviour Jesus Christ on the one hand, and the Pharisees and scribes on the other. And some people are tempted to say, 'Why do we bother with all that? What has all that got to do with me? Give me the simple, direct gospel message, that's all I want. I'm not interested in the scribes and Pharisees. I don't know what it's all about.' But that is to miss the whole point. Why did the Pharisees and scribes argue? Why did our Lord have to spend all that time with them? It is still the same answer. They had the wrong idea in their approach to God, and before our Lord could help them, before they would listen to the gospel, he had to make clear what was wrong.

And then look through the long running history of the years, and you find that men and women go on repeating this error. Look at the great period of the Protestant Reformation – what was the matter? What was it that Martin Luther had to do? It was the very thing that Isaiah is doing in this first chapter of his prophecy. There was the Church of Rome – organized, established religion, doing the wrong thing. And Luther's eyes were opened to that, he denounced this wrong approach. Organized religion has done this throughout the centuries and every reformation has been a denunciation of the wrong and then a proclamation of the true and the right way.

There are many who are genuinely disturbed today.

They can see that the times are out of joint. They can see that the world is in trouble. They are in trouble in their own personal lives but they say, 'What can I do?' And they begin to rush into some action and it is invariably wrong. Exactly like these people here! So in order to consider this, let us put it in the form of principles.

First, let us look for a moment at human ideas of how to get right with God. Men and women have been convicted and they say, 'All right, I must get to know God. I must be right with him. I accept your message, but how do I carry it out?'

Well, we can see how they do it. Instinctively, they do what the people of Judah and Jerusaiem had been doing, and that is what is so wrong. They begin to say, 'I must go in for good works. I can see that if I'm to be blessed by God I must live a good life. I've been rather negligent. I've been living a selfish life, a life of pleasure, and that's why things have gone wrong, that's why I'm in trouble. Now I've certainly been convicted, so I'm going to turn over a new leaf and start living a new life.' It is all here in Isaiah, in the imagery of taking these beasts to the temple – the burnt offerings of rams, and the fat of fed beasts, and the bullocks and lambs and he goats and so on.

In modern guise that is the same as doing good. 'I've been too selfish,' says someone. 'I must do some good. Is there a good cause? Ah, yes, freedom from famine – this campaign against hunger. Very well, I'll give a big donation! Now that's a good thing to do, that shows I'm no longer selfish! I'll do this because I'm concerned about these other people. I never used to do good things like that, but now I'm going to do more and more. I'm going to be a philanthropist and give alms in some shape or form. I'm sure that if I lead this good life, it will put me right with God!'

Good works, good actions. That is what men and women instinctively do, is it not? Then, in addition to good works, they take up religion: attendance at a place of worship, reading the Bible. 'You must do that,' they say. 'I think that must be the way. People have always done that!' So here they are, people who never went to a place of worship at all, who were not interested, and thought it a waste of time and very boring, starting to go to church because they feel that will put them right with God. They also begin to read the Bible and try to understand it.

Moreover, these people are not content with reading the Bible and praying and singing hymns – they add to what God has commanded us to do. Here in Isaiah we read that God says, 'The new moons and sabbaths, the calling of assemblies, I cannot away with; it is iniquity, even the solemn meeting. Your new moons and your appointed feasts my soul hateth: they are a trouble unto me; I am weary to bear them.' That is a reference to the fact that many of the children of Israel, who were rebelling so much against God and breaking his commandments so grievously, were still continuing to be highly religious.

Many people are still like this – scrupulously exact in religious observance, even adding their own rules to God's words. There are people who know nothing about trusting in simple faith to the death of Christ, who, indeed, pour scorn upon the doctrine of the atonement, but who are very devout and religious! They are not content with a simple, unadorned service, but are interested in postures and in attitudes, in ceremonies and in fastings. They get up at an unearthly hour, and are ever rushing to meetings and services, and they really believe that this is putting them right with God. They have an elaborate ritual about which you read nothing at all in the Bible. They have invented it. They are going beyond the Scriptures to show how religious they are. All that is 'the new moons and sabbaths', and all the rest of it, which God says his soul hates, which are a trouble to him and which he finds weary indeed to bear.

And then, finally, prayer. 'When ye spread forth your hands, I will hide mine eyes from you.' Even prayer! And the history of religion shows this very plainly. You can read of people in Tibet and other places with their prayer wheels. The wheel goes round and round and there is a prayer corresponding to every spoke and they spend hours and hours with their wheel working at this prayer ritual. Then there are others who pray with their beads. They count them and spend a great deal of time in these acts which they call 'acts of devotion'. They hold up their hands to God, praying to him in this elaborate manner, and are quite convinced that, as the result of this, God will accept them and forgive them. That is what men and women do instinctively.

I remember once preaching in Manchester on justification by faith, and at the close of the service a very honest and sincere young lady came to me. She had obviously missed the whole point of the sermon because she said, 'I'm a seeker, a seeker after God. I want to do the will of God. I want to be religious. If you tell me that I am to give up my post here in Manchester and forsake it all and my family with it, and go out and be a missionary in the heart of Africa, I'm ready to do it.'

'I have no doubt that you are,' I said, 'but the question I want to ask you is this: Are you prepared to do nothing so heroic, but just to start being a Christian in your job, where you are in Manchester?'

And she did not like it. Oh yes, people are prepared to make great sacrifices. There are many such people, and they are regarded, sometimes, as very fine Christians. They give up a great career with great possibilities. People say, 'Isn't it wonderful? That's Christianity! Look at the sacrifices they've made!' Other people go out of everyday life and become what is called 'religious', that is to say, they become monks or nuns or something like that. They go out of the world, out of all its pleasures and joys, leaving all the money, and they segregate themselves in order to be right with God. But these sacrifices do not put them right with God.

And that leads us to the second principle: Why are all these things rejected by God? Verse 11 begins with an extraordinary question: 'To what purpose is the multitude of your sacrifices unto me?' These words are so astounding that they have often been completely misunderstood. 'Aha,' says the modern critic of the Bible, 'I can explain that quite easily. That's the old fight between the prophet and the priest. The priests tell people to take offerings; the prophets say, "Don't do it, there's nothing in them." The priests and the prophets contradict one another. Why do you say that your Bible is inspired? How can I submit to a word that at one time says one thing, and at another time says the opposite?'

That is the argument of the so-called 'higher criticism'. How pathetic it is. There is no contradiction here at all. It was God who gave the commands about burnt offerings and sacrifices. You will find it all in the books of Leviticus and Numbers. God gave the people detailed instructions about the burnt offerings and the sacrifices and the blood of bulls and lambs and he goats. And God commanded the people to pray and to have feasts and fasts.

'Well,' you say, 'if it was God who commanded it, what does Isaiah mean by saying that God now says he cannot stand it and is prohibiting it? How do you reconcile these two things?'

There is no difficulty about the reconciliation because it is not what these people were doing that was wrong, it was the way in which they were doing it. What was wrong was the abuse of the right thing; it was the misunderstanding of the meaning of what God commanded. God is not here denouncing his own commandments, that is impossible. He is denouncing completely and utterly the people's whole view of it, and the use they were making of it.

The discovery of this truth was the thing that led to the

Protestant Reformation. There he was, that young monk Martin Luther, so disturbed and depressed, and he said: My life is a failure. I'm miserable. I don't know God, how can I know him? Well, the way to know God is to fast, to sweat in prayer, to give yourself to the religious life.

So Luther did that. But the more he fasted and prayed, the further away God seemed to be! What did he discover? That it is wrong to pray and fast and sweat? No! He discovered that it was his reliance upon these things that was wrong; it was his attitude towards them that was not right. And so his eyes were opened to the simple and glorious doctrine of justification by faith only.

But what does that mean? Again, let me put it in a number of principles. How is it that to live a good life, even to come to the house of God, even to read the Bible, even to pray, may mean that you are going further from God instead of getting nearer? What is wrong? Well, here are the things that are wrong. First of all, these things may be external only, they may not involve the heart. Our Lord once said, 'This people honoureth me with their lips, but their heart is far from me' (*Mark* 7:6). And, God knows, we all know something about that. We enjoy singing hymns, do we not?

> *Jesus, Thou joy of loving hearts,*
> *Thou fount of life, Thou light of men,*
> *From the best bliss that earth imparts,*
> *We turn unfilled to Thee again.*
> Bernard of Clairvaux

You may have often sung it, but did you mean it?

Our Lord himself put this to the Pharisees in a terrible, final denunciation that makes one shudder:

Woe unto you, scribes and Pharisees, hypocrites! for ye make clean the outside of the cup and of the platter,

[127]

*but within they are full of extortion and excess.
Thou blind Pharisee, cleanse first that which is
within the cup and platter, that the outside of them
may be clean also. Woe unto you, scribes and
Pharisees, hypocrites! for ye are like unto whited
sepulchres, which indeed appear beautiful outward,
but are within full of dead men's bones, and of all
uncleanness. Even so ye also outwardly appear righteous unto men, but within ye are full of hypocrisy and
iniquity. Woe unto you, scribes and Pharisees,
hypocrites! because ye build the tombs of the
prophets, and garnish the sepulchres of the righteous,
and say, If we had been in the days of our fathers, we
would not have been partakers with them in the
blood of the prophets. Wherefore ye be witnesses
unto yourselves, that ye are the children of them
which killed the prophets. Fill ye up then the measure
of your fathers. Ye serpents, ye generation of vipers,
how can ye escape the damnation of hell?*

(*Matt.* 23:25–33)

It is the Son of God speaking, the incarnation of God's
love, and that is how he spoke to them! They were doing
all these things! Excellent in religious practice, yes, but it
was external and mechanical, and the inside was rotten.
That is the first charge.

Secondly, how utterly superficial it is, this attitude
towards God and true worship. Here it is again, also from
Matthew 23: 'Woe unto you, scribes and Pharisees,
hypocrites! for ye pay tithe of mint and anise and
cummin, and have omitted the weightier matters of the
law, judgment, mercy, and faith: these ought ye to have
done, and not to leave the other undone' (*Matt.* 23:23).
You see, that was so typical of the Pharisees. They
thought they were very righteous; they were tithing all
these things – they were experts on details – and they

thought: 'As long as we are doing this we are right with God.'

Thirdly, people who think that these things are all you have to do, always, of course, regard them as meritorious in and of themselves. As long as you go to the early morning service, you are all right; as long as you go through the ceremony and the ritual, you are all right! They see the activity as an end in and of itself; they go through the performance and think all is well. They have never seen that the purpose of all these things that God has ordained is to bring us into a relationship with himself. They are doing their duty, and as long as they have done their duty, they think all is well. That was precisely the trouble with the Pharisees.

But let me give you the fourth charge. The real trouble with men and women who think that this is the way to be right with God is that they are really not thinking of God at all, they are only thinking of themselves. Our Lord has again put this perfectly once and for ever in his famous picture of the Pharisee and the tax collector who went up into the temple to pray. 'The Pharisee stood and prayed thus with himself' – exactly! It was all with himself – 'God' – Oh, yes, he is bound to mention the name of God. But God is an aside, as it were. 'He prayed thus with himself, God, I thank thee, that I am not as other men are, extortioners, unjust, adulterers, or even as this publican. I fast twice in the week, I give tithes of all that I possess.'

The tax collector was there, but '. . . standing afar off, would not lift up so much as his eyes unto heaven, but smote upon his breast, saying, God be merciful to me a sinner. I tell you,' said Jesus, 'this man' – the tax-collector – 'went down to his house justified rather than the other: for every one that exalteth himself shall be abased; and he that humbleth himself shall be exalted' (*Luke* 18:11–14).

You see, these men and women are putting themselves right. They are filled with pride and they thank God that they are so religious. They say that they are doing so much good and they boast of it. I know many people who never go to a place of worship, but who say, 'I'm all right, look what I'm doing. You people talk; I'm the *doer*! I'm giving my donations. I'm doing a lot of good.' Yes, they are exactly like the Pharisee. But, I suppose the perfect illustration of all this is none other than the apostle Paul himself before his conversion. How proud he was of his righteousness and goodness! And the moment you set off along this track, thinking that your good works or your religion or your prayers or your Bible reading or your church attendance, or anything else, are going to save you, you always end up in pride and self-satisfaction, which is an abomination in the sight of God.

But we must go further. God condemns all this religiosity because it is not what he has asked for. God is not interested merely in some mechanical actions. Listen to the apostle putting it to the Romans: 'Brethren,' he says, 'my heart's desire and prayer to God for Israel is, that they might be saved. For I bear them record that they have a zeal of God, but not according to knowledge. For they being ignorant of God's righteousness, and going about to establish their own righteousness, have not submitted themselves unto the righteousness of God' (*Rom.* 10:1–3). Paul is saying, in effect, 'I am ready to admit that my fellow countrymen are zealous. They are very religious and in a sense they are very good people, but the tragedy is that it is not what God has asked, it is what they think he has asked. They have not submitted themselves to God's righteousness; they are establishing their own righteousness.' And that is what all such people are doing.

Let me again quote to you that case of poor Saul, the first king of Israel. Oh, the tragedy of that man! What terrible words the prophet Samuel had to utter to him! 'Hath the Lord as great delight in burnt offerings and sacrifices, as in obeying the voice of the Lord? Behold, to obey is better than sacrifice, and to hearken than the fat of rams. For rebellion is as the sin of witchcraft, and stubbornness is as iniquity and idolatry. Because thou hast rejected the word of the Lord, he hath also rejected thee from being king' (*1 Sam.* 15:22–23). It is perfectly clear that Saul thought he was doing a very good thing. He said, 'The people spared the best of the sheep and of the oxen, to sacrifice unto the Lord thy God.' Yes, but God had not asked him to do that! God had told him to destroy everything – men, women, children, all the animals – nothing was to be left.

Saul says: Ah, but we've kept the best. We want to give an offering.

God says: I don't want your offering. I want your obedience.

The prophet Hosea puts it like this: 'I desired mercy, and not sacrifice; and the knowledge of God more than burnt offerings' (*Hos.* 6:6). God wants the right use of these things. He does not want our ideas of righteousness. He does not want all our good works and all our offerings and ceremonial. He wants our hearts, our obedience, our utter subjection to him. So anything we try to give as a substitute for that is an abomination in his sight. And the moment you begin to realize what God wants, you will very soon realize that all you have been doing is unworthy.

Listen to Isaiah in another place: 'All our righteousnesses are as filthy rags' (*Isa.* 64:6). Or take it in the words of St Paul. Here was a Pharisee, a Hebrew of the Hebrews, of the tribe of Benjamin, circumcised on the eighth day, knowing all about the law, and keeping it better than anybody else, a proud, self-righteous Pharisee, a wonderful fellow! But then his eyes were opened and he wrote, 'But what things were gain to me, those I counted loss for Christ. Yea doubtless, and I count all things but loss' – dung and refuse – 'for the excellency of the knowledge of Christ Jesus my Lord' (*Phil.* 3:7–8). All Paul's goodness, all his religiosity, all his praying, all he had ever done, was manure, it was putrefying, it was filthy. Fancy my ever thinking that that was going to be acceptable in God's sight! What unutterable folly! That is what God is saying here through the prophet Isaiah.

So what men and women do instinctively is entirely useless; it is all wrong. And lastly, I ask: Why do they behave like this? Why is it that people will do all these things – give up their careers and go to the heart of Africa, make sacrifices – do anything except believe the simple gospel? Why will they do anything rather than fall at the foot of the cross of Christ and give their hearts to him? Why will they accept anything from the Scriptures except the statement, 'Ye must be born again' (*John* 3:7)? Why does that infuriate them? Why is the cross an annoyance to them? Why is it that when they begin to feel that things are wrong and they want to put them right, they immediately go and do the wrong thing? What is the matter with them?

I will tell you – it is that there is nothing right with them. That is the trouble. That is the trouble with every one of us: we are all wrong and there is no health in us. We have already seen that in Isaiah. 'From the sole of the foot even unto the head there is no soundness in it.' As the result of sin and the fall, men and women are rotten; they have fallen completely. And they prove that, not only by sinning and rebelling against God, by getting themselves into trouble and continuing, even when they are punished, but when they are awakened, they prove it still more by instinctively doing the wrong thing. What fools they are!

We can put it like this: people behave in this way because ultimately the essence of sin is pride and self-confidence. That is our main trouble. We have already seen this. We start off by thinking that we have great minds and brains and that with our thinking and philosophy we can find out what is wrong about life and the world, and that we can put it right! But we are beginning to see that we are not quite as clever as we thought we were, we are now prepared to submit to revelation. But even then our pride rises up because here, as the next step shows, in our pride and self-confidence we think that we know what it is that God wants, what it is to be religious, and how God is to be pleased. We do not stop to say, 'Now what does the word of the Lord say? Doesn't the Bible tell me about the way of salvation?' We do not consider that. We think we know, and off we go along the wrong road, exactly like the children of Israel.

We think we know what needs to be done and we are mad enough to think we can do it! Having been awakened, and having now understood that there is a God, we think that we have got it in us to please him. 'Very well,' we say, 'now let me see, I want a helpful book. Ah, here is the very book I want: *The Imitation of Christ*! I am to set about imitating Christ. He pleased God; very well, so can I. What did he do? Right, I'm going to do the same.'

That is exactly what men and women do in their unutterable pride and folly, in their idiotic self-confidence. They think they can justify themselves before God who 'is light, and in him is no darkness at all' (*1 John* 1:5). They think they can make themselves so pure and so clean that they can stand the gaze of God! That is just madness. It is pride and self-confidence to the nth degree.

Another way in which this pride and self-confidence show themselves is that we think that we can fool God with our hypocrisy. We really think that we can pass it off. We go on living more or less as we were, but we 'do good' and say to ourselves, 'Well, of course, that good work I've done, that philanthropic action, will cancel out everything. I know I'm not perfect, but look at what I've done! There it is in red letters – my donation, my zeal, my religion!' And we think that God will only look at one side of the ledger and not see the other. It works with our fellow human beings; we can get away with it with them.

We are all hypocrites, and very clever hypocrites. Because people think we are better than we are, we presume God does too. The attitude is: 'I'll balance evil with good. I'll square the books and everything will be all right.' We are proud enough to think that that will really work with God and that an occasional burnt offering and sacrifice with an occasional appearing in his house – Easter Sunday morning perhaps – will cover everything. We really believe that. That is why we do these things.

What tragic folly it is. Do you know the answer to all that? Our Lord once said to these selfsame Pharisees, 'You are they which justify ourselves before men; but God knoweth your hearts: for that which is highly esteemed among men is abomination in the sight of God' (*Luke* 16:15). That includes all our goodness, all our righteousness, all our gifts, all our burnt offerings, all our sacrifices. The world says, 'Isn't it wonderful!' But it is an 'abomination in the sight of God'. 'Except your righteousness shall exceed the righteousness of the scribes and Pharisees, ye shall in no case enter into the kingdom of heaven' (*Matt.* 5:20).

Are you awakened to the state of your soul? Have you realized that you have to die and face God in the judgment? Are you beginning to feel that you must be right with God? That is good, but what are you to do? There is only one thing – listen for your life to the word of God. Do not go off on that false track; do not think that you can do anything for yourself – you cannot. Believe the word of God here and now, hearken diligently and obey it.

Not the labours of my hands
Can fulfil Thy law's demands;
Could my zeal no respite know,
Could my tears for ever flow,
All for sin could not atone;
Thou must save, and Thou alone.
Augustus Toplady

9: *God's Final Word*

*Wash you, make you clean; put away the evil of your doings
from before mine eyes; cease to do evil; learn to do well; seek
judgment, relieve the oppressed, judge the fatherless, plead for
the widow. Come now, and let us reason together, saith the
Lord: though your sins be as scarlet, they shall be as white as
snow; though they be red like crimson, they shall be as wool.*
Isaiah 1:16–18

In Isaiah 1, you remember, the prophet, at the very outset
of his great prophetic message, gives a kind of synopsis of
the whole of the message which God had given to him to
deliver to his fellow countrymen. He prophesied to them
at a time of trouble and difficulty. Had there been no
difficulties, there would never have been any prophets.
God raised up this succession of men to address the
nation when they were going astray, when they were
wandering away from him. And the whole object of their
message was to indicate to them the source of their
troubles, and finally, of course, to call them to repentance
and to indicate God's readiness to receive them, and the
blessings which he always has ready and waiting for a
truly repentant people.

So we have been working our way through that introduction, and we have seen that the main subject has
inevitably been the whole question of sin. The nation was
in trouble because of sin, and what the prophet does here,
as the whole of the Bible does, is analyse sin, show it for
what it is, display it in its real colours. And we have found
that the prophet has been saying quite a number of things
about sin. He has shown us that sin is rebellion, folly and
madness, and turns men and women into hypocrites.

But the ultimate truth about men and women who are

in sin is that they are utterly unreasonable, they are completely inexcusable and without any defence at all. We see this in the verses to which we now turn, verses which, I venture to suggest, are God's final word to unrepentant sinners. The way in which he addresses them is this: 'Come now, and let us reason together, saith the Lord: though your sins be as scarlet, they shall be as white as snow; though they be red like crimson, they shall be as wool.' This is a most extraordinary statement, perhaps one of the most astonishing things that God ever says to men and women.

You notice that God makes an appeal: 'Come now.' Is it not astonishing that the great, almighty and eternal God, existing from eternity to eternity, self-sufficient in himself, triune, the God who made humanity and all things, should appeal to us, that he should call upon us and ask us to listen? Is it not one of the most wonderful facts in this whole universe, that God should bother with us at all? He could live without us; he did exist without us. He is not dependent upon us, we have no contribution to make, and yet he appeals to us. But it is still more wonderful that he should appeal to people like these children of Israel – these people who, though he had nourished them and brought them up, rebelled against him; these people who, as it were, had spat in his face, spurned his voice and desecrated all the sanctities; these people who were guilty of the various things that we have seen as we have considered this whole picture. Here is the amazing thing, that God should still say, 'Come', that he did not abandon them and hand them over to an ultimate reprobate mind from which there is no deliverance, and blast them to eternal perdition.

But it is the whole basis and foundation of the Christian gospel that God, the almighty, ever blessed God, so loved this world as it is that 'He gave his only begotten Son.' Indeed, the whole message of the Bible is epitomized in this one word, 'Come.' Here we see God appealing to men and women. He began to do it in the Garden of Eden. When Adam and Eve sinned, God came down into the Garden as his custom was, and they ran away and hid. But God said, 'Adam, where art thou?' It was 'Come' – Come and speak to me. Come and listen to me. Come and say what you have got to say for yourself. And this is the great message of the prophets, the message of the apostles, the message of all the preachers in the Christian Church throughout the running centuries. It says to a world in sin and shame and sorrow: 'Wait a moment. Come. Listen.'

But above all, of course, it is the great word in the preaching of our blessed Lord and Saviour himself, and this is the miracle and the marvel of grace. 'Come unto me, all ye that labour and are heavy laden, and I will give you rest' (*Matt.* 11:28). 'Come.' It is a great appeal to us; it is an announcement that God has not finished with us, that he still has something to say to us. It tells us that he has not abandoned us though we are guilty of all the folly that we have been considering. That is the first thing that strikes us about this invitation.

The second is this: these words of Isaiah are an appeal from God, and a call from God, to come and to reason – 'Come now, and let us reason together, saith the Lord.' This means that the almighty, eternal God, against whom we have sinned and rebelled, stoops down to our level and says in effect, 'Come, let us have a discussion. I have spoken to you. I have sent my prophets to you. I have appealed to you, but you do not listen. Come,' he says, 'I will come down. Come, let us have it right out. You put your case and I will put mine. Come, let us reason together.' It is a call, an invitation to a debate, to a frank statement of the two sides, giving us complete freedom to say what we want to say, to bring out all our objections and all our troubles and problems, a complete freedom to state our case to God.

And here we see once more the indescribable fairness of God in his teaching and his message. Let no one represent this as God dragooning us – he does not do that. In his sovereign act of salvation, God does not dragoon people, he persuades them. Let us not mis-understand the great doctrine which tells us that we are saved by grace alone. We are not knocked on the head; we are not bludgeoned. Here is a wonderful display of the final reasonableness of God.

But think, too, of God's infinite condescension. He who made all things, and needs nothing from anybody, he who has the right and the power to do anything he wills, nevertheless humbles himself, as it were, to meet people like these recalcitrant children of Israel. He says: Come along, then, I am allowing you to speak. Let me hear every argument that you can produce. I am ready to listen.

The ultimate condescension was when God 'sent forth his Son, made of a woman, made under the law, to redeem them that were under the law' (*Gal.* 4:4). There he is, look at him – Jesus of Nazareth, Son of God, buffeted by the crowds, Pharisees and scribes putting clever questions to him, arguing and debating, and he humbled himself to that. He was ready to enter into this process of reasoning. He took upon himself, not only the form of a man, but the form of a servant – the meek, and lowly, the humble Jesus!

It is all here, in the words, 'Come now, let us reason together, saith the Lord.' This is a perfect statement of the essence of the Christian gospel of salvation. But we do not leave it there, because in this expression, 'Come now,' there is yet a further element, and I would be a dishonest expositor if I did not give it. There is another element in this expression and that is the element of challenge. Yes, God is going to give us an opportunity to say anything we want to say, but remember that once you have said it, you have said it, and you will never be able to open your mouth again. God says: Very well, you do not listen to my message, you are not impressed by what I am saying, so produce all your arguments and I will reply to them, and then what will you have to say?

In other words, God is here bringing everything to a head. It is his final word. He says: No more bothering about, let us come to the point. I have sent my messengers, I have put the arguments, and you take no notice. Very well, now let us have a final clearing up of this matter.

It is all in this invitation. And in putting it in this way, of course, God is unfolding and unmasking the final unreasonableness of men and women in sin: the fact that there is nothing whatsoever to be said for them. Christians are those who have come to see that they have nothing to say. They give up. They give in and say, 'All right, I've been talking. I've been arguing. I've been expressing my difficulties and my problems. I've no more to say.' Like Job, they put their hands upon their mouths (*Job* 40:4) and see what fools they have been in all that they have been trying to say. They are driven into a corner, and there is no reply, no argument, no plea. They submit entirely and completely to God's word – as we saw in our consideration of verse 10.

So let us look at this as God puts it before us here through the prophet Isaiah. What is this argument that people are persuaded of when they become Christians? What is it that finally breaks down every resistance and opposition and makes them say, 'I have nothing more to say, I believe'? And we can put the answer in the form of three principles.

The first is the rightness of God's demands on us. These things need to be proved because men and women are disputing them. They ask, 'What right has God to do this?' It was the old temptation which the devil put at the beginning. 'Hath God said, Ye shall not eat of every tree of the garden?' What right has God to say that? There is an objection, a feeling that it is not right. But here God justifies his demands upon us. 'Come,' he says, 'let us

reason together.' He says, 'Wash you, make you clean;
put away the evil of your doings from before mine eyes;
cease to do evil; learn to do well; seek judgment, relieve
the oppressed, judge the fatherless, plead for the widow.'
These are God's demands on us, and they are right, they
are righteous. But on what grounds?

The Bible is full of answers to that question. God is our
maker – 'It is he that hath made us, and not we ourselves'
(*Psa.* 100:3). He has given us life and being and all things.
He created us for himself, for his own pleasure. We were
not involved. We were not consulted. We have not produced ourselves, clever though we are! God made us and
he made us in a particular manner and for a particular
purpose. He made us that we might have companionship
with him.

God made Adam in his own image in order that he
might govern God's own universe. That man was to be
the lord of creation and he was made obviously for the
enjoyment of God. And God was perfectly at liberty to do
this. He made man and he endowed him with certain
faculties and with certain powers. He gave him a mind.
He gave him reason and understanding. He made him
essentially different from the animals. Animals live
according to their lusts, their instincts, their desires; not
so man. He was given a critical faculty. He was given the
power of looking on at himself and of making estimates.
He was able to curb and to control himself. He was different, not a part of creation but the lord of it. God, in other
words, gave something of his own power. He could not
have paid a greater compliment.

And not only that, God gave freedom. Man, as he was
originally made, was absolutely free, with free will,
complete freedom of choice. And not only that, God set
before man a very glorious possibility. He told him that if
he obeyed the commandments of God, he would be
glorified and would never die at all.

That is how God made man and set him in this world.

[140]

And God here argues that he has a perfect right, therefore, to lay down conditions for men and women and to
make demands of them. There is nothing derogatory in
that. There is nothing derogatory in asking them to
acknowledge the lordship of the Almighty. We recognize
that. There must be authority, there must be government,
and therefore there must be recognition of it. Well,
multiply all that by infinity and there we are under God. It
is no insult to finite human beings to ask them to obey the
almighty God.

But we can go beyond that. What God demands of us is
something that is essentially right and good in and of itself.
I am thinking in particular of the Ten Commandments.
These are divided into two Tables. The first Table is with
respect to our relationship to God – how we shall worship
God and honour him, not taking his name in vain, not
bowing down to any graven image, not breaking God's
day, but honouring it. What is wrong in that? What is
wrong in bowing down in worship before the everlasting
God? It is essentially right.

But then come to the second Table. Honour your
father and mother – have you any objection to that? You
shall not kill; you shall not steal; you shall not commit
adultery. What is wrong with these things? Go on: You
shall not covet; you shall not bring a false accusation.
What is your objection? Is there anything wrong in God
making demands like this upon us?

Or take God's commands as they are put here in Isaiah:
'Wash you, make you clean.' God wants us to be clean.
He wants us to be pure. Have you any objection to that?
As David puts it in the fifty-first psalm: 'Thou desirest
truth in the inward parts' (verse 6). Would you not like to
have a clean heart, a heart which never has a vile imagination and never an impure thought? Would you not like to
have it? What is wrong with it? That is what God wants.
'Learn to do well,' he says, 'seek judgment, relieve the
oppressed, judge the fatherless, plead for the widow.'

If only everybody were practising these things, this would be a perfect world. If only everybody lived the Ten Commandments, the moral law and the Sermon on the Mount, there would be no threat of war; there would be no making of bombs. The whole world would not be in a state of tension and alarm. No, if everybody lived as God asks us to live, the world would be paradise; it would be perfect.

Consider, therefore, the essential rightness of God's demands. 'Come now, come let us reason together.' Where is the counsel for the opposition, for the defence? Where are you? What have you to say? Where is your objection to the righteous demands of God? Why do you object to having 'truth in your inward parts'? Why do you object to being told that you should have a clean heart? What is the objection to the life that was lived by the Son of God himself while he was in this world? There is none. Answer if you can.

There, then, is the first thing, but let me go on to the second. Having established the righteousness of God's demands upon us and their essential rightness, let us go on to consider the essential justice of God's punishment of us for our failure and sin. That is the matter at issue because here he is threatening punishment. He threatens punishment in the whole of the Bible. If you take the element of punishment out, how much is left? There never would have been a salvation were it not for punishment; there never would have been the cross on Calvary were it not for the wrath of God against sin. These things are indissolubly linked.

Consider also the righteousness of God's judgment. He says: Come, I have been threatening you. I have been telling you what is going to happen. Now then, produce all your objections, anything that you can think of. Here is my case against you, answer it who can.

To begin with, God has a right to be the judge of all the earth, and he *is* the judge of all the earth. He has the right to it, of course, for the reasons I have already given: that he is our maker; he is the great lawgiver. Not only that, God has made it plain from the very beginning that he will punish sin and disobedience, rebellion and transgression. Take our forefathers, take Adam and Eve in the Garden of Eden. God made it very plain to them. He said: If you live according to my commandments, I will bless you and you will have that wonderful gift of glorification and immortality. But if you eat of this tree of the knowledge of good and evil, 'dying you shall die', you will be driven out of the Garden.

God has established the principle of judgment and he has told us exactly what the terms of the judgment are. Could anything be fairer? If God suddenly landed judgment upon us without our ever having been forewarned, then it would be unjust, but God has told us. We can make no plea of ignorance, the law is open before us. God says: I will judge you in terms of what I made you, and what I have asked of you.

So let us look at ourselves in the judgment. Let each of us look at our hands and at our heart. God's verdict is this: 'Wash you, make you clean.' What about our actions? 'Put away the evil of your doings from before mine eyes; cease to do evil; learn to do well.' Let us examine ourselves. God made man 'a living soul' (*Gen.* 2:7). Men and women are not animals; they have souls; they have eternal spirits. They are meant for God and for life and companionship with God. They are meant to reflect something of God's glory as they live in this world. They are meant to live that life which is indicated in the Ten Commandments and elsewhere. But what have we done? What is the result? What do we find when we examine ourselves in the light of these things? What of your soul? What of your knowledge of God? What of your love? Do you not see the need of washing? Do you not see the stains, the mud and the mire of the world, covering us without and within? 'There is no health in

us,' we read in the general confession in the Prayer Book.
That is how we shall be judged – on our attitude to God,
and then our life as we have lived it.

Isaiah makes this clear for us in his account of his great
vision. It is so difficult for us to visualize the judgment, so
difficult for us to visualize God. And today's clever men
and women are trying to tell us that we cannot, that God
is 'depth', or something like that. Who can understand
such a thought? It is nonsense! The Bible tries to help us
by painting pictures. We have looked already at Isaiah's
vision: read that great sixth chapter of Isaiah again. Have
you ever visualized yourself in the presence of God?
Isaiah merely had a dim and distant vision. Can you
imagine what it is to stand before the burning fire and
look on that light? Surely there is only one thing to say:
'There is none righteous, no, not one' (*Rom.* 3:10).

Before you and I can stand in the presence of God, we
must be clean. 'Who shall ascend into the hill of the Lord?
or who shall stand in his holy place? He that hath clean
hands, and a pure heart' (*Psa.* 24:3–4). Have you got
those things? Can you cleanse yourself? 'Wash you, make
you clean.' Get rid of the stains, get rid of the blots.
Cleanse your heart, you unrighteous. 'Put away the evil
of your doings from before mine eyes; cease to do evil.'
'Rend your heart, and not your garments' (*Joel* 2:13).
That is the demand of God. Can you get rid of the guilt of
your past sins? Can you purify your heart and renew a
right spirit within yourself? Can you stop sinning? Can
you do good? Can you learn to do well? Can you live life
as Christ lived it? Can you honour the Sermon on the
Mount? You are called upon to do it, and if you cannot,
you are condemned; you are a failure; you are lost.

What have you to say? You believe in free will? You
believe in the power of human beings? You think that
men and women can make themselves fit to stand in the
presence of God? Very well, that is what you must produce – clean hands and a pure heart. But can you do it?

Can anybody do it? 'How should a man be just with God?' (*Job* 9:2). 'Can the Ethiopian change his skin, or the leopard his spots?' (*Jer.* 13:23). Can you, in the words of Shakespeare, get rid of these 'damned spots' – the blood that in some shape or form is upon every one of us. 'Out, out, damned spot!' Can you do it? If you cannot, you cannot stand in the presence of God.

That is what God demands. God himself is light and holy and pure. In him is no darkness, and he cannot admit into his presence anything that is unlike that. It is impossible, of course. Darkness cannot dwell with light, impurity cannot dwell with purity, they are self-contradictory. The purity, the light of God, shrivels everything else into nothing. And the holy God announces his judgment. As the result of the rebellion and sin and the fall, men and women are unclean – 'There is none righteous, no, not one.'

And when God announces his judgment there is no plea. King David, when he had repented after his great sin, said, 'Against thee, thee only, have I sinned, and done this evil in thy sight: that thou mightest be justified when thou speakest, and be clear when thou judgest' (*Psa.* 51:4). 'Oh God,' said David in effect, 'I'm not trying to justify myself, I want to justify you. I deserve nothing but damnation. I've been an adulterer, a murderer. God, I've sinned against you and have nothing to offer on my own behalf as a plea. I want to justify you when you speak, and clear you when you judge.'

That is a man who has seen the truth, who has repented. That is a man who says, 'There is no reply. I've reasoned with you, Oh Lord, and there is nothing more to be said. I give in. You are just if you blot me out for ever and ever.'

So, then, we have seen the rightness of God's demands and the justice of God's judgment and punishment. But the thing that finally silences everybody is the grace of God's offer, and that is why verses 16–18 must be taken together. Listen, God says. Come, let us go on, I have not finished. You are silent, you cannot speak now. Of course not! My demands are right. My justice is right and absolutely just, but come, listen to me, we have not finished. 'Come now, and let us reason together.' My case is not ended, I have more to say. I have grace to offer you. 'Though your sins be as scarlet, they shall be as white as snow; though they be red like crimson, they shall be as wool.'

What does God mean? Oh, this is his final word to us. When he has convicted us and convinced us of the righteousness of his demands and the justice of his punishment, and we see ourselves lost and damned, God comes to us and says: Listen. Give in to me. Admit. Confess. Repent. Cast yourself on my mercy. Give up, stop pleading, stop excusing; stop trying to deceive me with your hypocrisy. Acknowledge your sin and your guilt. Fall before me in utter self-condemnation. Say unto me, as that poor tax collector said, who went up into the temple to pray, 'God be merciful to me a sinner' (*Luke* 18:13). And you know what will happen? 'Though your sins be as scarlet, they shall be as white as snow; though they be red like crimson, they shall be as wool.' This is his offer.

If we acknowledge our sin and submit to 'the word of the Lord, and to the law of our God', he will give us free and full forgiveness. He says that though our sins have been so deeply dyed as to be scarlet, they will be dealt with in such a way that they will be as white as snow. Though we have sinned until our sin is as red as crimson, it shall be as white as wool. This is the amazing thing that God offers us in the blessed gospel of his Son. Isaiah here gives us just a prophecy of it, it is nothing else. What God is saying here is this: 'If we confess our sins, he is faithful and just to forgive us our sins, and to cleanse us from all unrighteousness' (*1 John* 1:9). Here is free and full forgiveness, our sins blotted out as a thick cloud and cast into the sea of God's forgetfulness, cancelled out of the ledgers of heaven once and for ever, as if they had never been there.

Oh, I do want to bring this out to you. Even if you are the worst and the deepest of sinners, I am proud and happy and rejoice in being able to tell you that your sins can be forgiven as fully and as freely as those of the best person. You may have touched every depth of hell, you may have committed every sin that has ever been heard of; your sins may be as scarlet, but I assure you, in the name of God, that if you but recognize and acknowledge it and give up and believe on the Son of God, they will become as white as snow. It will all be entirely removed, with free, full, absolute forgiveness. That is what he is offering.

What else? Well, in addition to forgiveness, there is justification. This is a very wonderful thing. I am so glad that Isaiah puts it like this; it is to me the greatest comfort of all. He does not say: 'Though your sins be as scarlet, I'll just erase them and you will not be able to see them any longer.' No, no, there is a transformation here: 'They shall be as white as snow; though they be red like crimson, they shall be as wool.' Justification means that when I believe in Christ, God takes all that is evil in me and puts it on his Son, and it has been punished in him. And then he takes the righteousness of his own Son and puts it on me. I have a robe of whiteness, of pure whiteness like snow, as white as wool; this is the righteousness of Christ. It does not matter what you have been before, if you have seen your sin and your hopelessness and are a believer in the Lord Jesus Christ, God now looks upon you as if you had never sinned at all! He has blotted out what you were – your old self died with Christ (*Rom.* 6:6) and is no longer in existence. God has put this robe of righteousness upon you, and when he looks at you, he does not see you, but Christ covering you with his perfect, spotless robe of righteousness.

What else? Well, he renews us, making us new men and

women; and as our Father, he begins to bless us. He says: I will put a new nature into you. I will make you 'partakers of the divine nature' (2 *Pet.* 1:4), and there is no evil or sin in that. I will give you a new start and a new life, and I will put my Spirit in you and I will lead you on, and eventually receive you unto myself.

But the most wonderful thing about it all is not only what God offers to do for us, it is the amazing way which he made so that he could do it. How can God turn these sins that are as scarlet and make them as white as snow? How does he take my sins which are red like crimson and turn them into the purity of wool? How does he do it? I know he is God, the Creator, and I know he is almighty. But how can he do this? And there is only one answer. He did it by sending his only begotten Son into this world. His Son left heaven, and took human nature. He humbled himself, taking the form of a servant, and endured the contradiction of sinners against himself. In this world, he lived a life like yours and mine. He suffered endless indignities and buffetings. His love for you and me took him to the Garden of Gethsemane where he was sweating drops of blood in this terrible struggle to turn the scarlet into snow and the crimson into the whiteness of wool.

How is it done? How is the scarlet turned into the whiteness of snow and the crimson into the whiteness of wool? And the answer is the alchemy of Gethsemane, the blood of Jesus Christ and the sweat; and then the cross, the shame and the suffering, the ignominy, the mocking of the crowd, the crown of thorns, everything that happened on that cross on Calvary's hill. That is what it cost; that is what made it all possible; that is the divine miracle that changes the scarlet into the whiteness of snow. And so God is able to make this free offer.

I must have clean hands. I must have a pure heart. I cannot do it. Have you not tried? We have all tried, and none of us has succeeded and never will, and yet without them I cannot stand before God. Oh, how can I cleanse myself, my hands, my heart, my spirit, my whole being? There is only one way. Listen: 'Have mercy upon me, O God, according to thy lovingkindness: according unto the multitude of thy tender mercies blot out my transgressions. Wash me throughly from mine iniquity, and cleanse me from my sin' – I cannot do it – 'Purge me with hyssop, and I shall be clean: wash me, and I shall be whiter than snow . . . Create in me a clean heart, O God; and renew a right spirit within me' (*Psa.* 51:1–2, 7, 10). There is the cry of the Old Testament, the cry of David in sin, the cry of every condemned sinner. We can but cry out to God for mercy and for compassion, and when we do he will point us to his dear Son and say: There is the answer, believe in him.

Is it true? Is it enough?

> *His blood can make the foulest clean,*
> *His blood availed for me.*

My privilege is to tell you this:

> *There is a fountain filled with blood*
>   *Drawn from Immanuel's veins;*
> *And sinners, plunged beneath that flood,*
>   *Lose all their guilty stains.*
>   William Cowper

Have you heard God's invitation: 'Come now, let us reason together'? You have heard his demands; you have heard the terms of judgment. Where do you stand? Can you justify yourself? Have you any excuse? Have you anything to say?

Listen to what God says to you, and say to him:

Just as I am, without one plea
But that Thy blood was shed for me,
And that Thou bidd'st me come to Thee,
     O Lamb of God, I come.
                         Charlotte Elliott

If you have never come before, come now. Then you will
know that one day you will be with a shining bright
crowd of people of all nations and kindreds and tongues,
with amazing white robes, and somebody will say, 'Who
are these? Who is that?'

And one of the angels will answer, 'Oh, that is the man,
the woman, who on a certain day suddenly saw the vileness, saw the spots, the blots, the uncleanness, the
foulness, the helplessness, and saw the condemnation of
God. And there and then that woman, that man, heard
God's offer and accepted it and they washed their robes
in the blood of the Lamb.'

Just as I am, and waiting not
To rid my soul of one dark blot,
To Thee, whose blood can cleanse each spot,
     O Lamb of God, I come.

TITLES BY
D. MARTYN LLOYD-JONES
AVAILABLE FROM
THE BANNER OF TRUTH TRUST

ROMANS SERIES:
The Gospel of God (1:1–32)
ISBN 0 85151 467 7, 408 pp.
The Righteous Judgment of God (2:1–3:20)
ISBN 0 85151 545 2, 240 pp.
Atonement and Justification (3:20–4:25)
ISBN 0 85151 034 5, 272 pp.
Assurance (5:1–21)
ISBN 0 85151 050 7, 384 pp.
The New Man (6:1–23)
ISBN 0 85151 158 9, 328 pp.
The Law (7:1–8:4)
ISBN 0 85151 180 5, 372 pp.
The Sons of God (8:5–17)
ISBN 0 85151 207 0, 400 pp.
Final Perseverance (8:17–39)
ISBN 0 85151 231 3, 460 pp.
God's Sovereign Purpose (9:1–33)
ISBN 0 85151 579 7, 344 pp.
Saving Faith (10:1–21)
ISBN 0 85151 737 4, 411 pp.
To God's Glory (11:1–36)
ISBN 0 85151 748 X, 304 pp.

'Dr Lloyd-Jones is a great biblical theologian but the reader will be impressed afresh by the strong experimental note in his theology.'

The Evangelical Quarterly

'It is solid fare that is presented, but with passion and fervour, with simplicity and clarity.'

The Expository Times

'The didactic style that proves so attractive in his pulpit utterances is equally effective in the written page.'

Free Church of Scotland Monthly Record

'Over the years Dr Lloyd-Jones has given us many things but this [vol 4] is surely the best yet . . . Dr Lloyd-Jones' expository sermons on Romans are thorough, magisterial, warm-hearted, earnest and energetic. '

Church of England Newspaper

EPHESIANS SERIES:
God's Ultimate Purpose (1:1–23)
ISBN 0 85151 272 0, 448 pp.
God's Way of Reconciliation (2:1–22)
ISBN 0 85151 299 2, 480 pp.
The Unsearchable Riches of Christ (3:1–21)
ISBN 0 85151 293 3, 320 pp.
Christian Unity (4:1–16)
ISBN 0 85151 312 3, 280 pp.
Darkness and Light (4:17–5:17)
ISBN 0 85151 343 3, 464 pp.
Life in the Spirit (5:18–6:9)
ISBN 0 85151 194 5, 372 pp.
The Christian Warfare (6:10–13)
ISBN 0 85151 243 7, 376 pp.
The Christian Soldier (6:10–20)
ISBN 0 85151 258 5, 368 pp.

(Not available in the USA)

'Characteristically rich in insight, inspiration and interpretation, reflecting his long years of preaching and pastoral experience . . . Even in printed form these sermons reveal the authority of the man who preached them and the greater authority of his message.'
Church of England Newspaper

'Good old-fashioned theological preaching of this kind is a healthy antidote to the superficiality of many modern sermons.'
Scottish Journal of Theology

'If you have grown weak on shallow teaching and fuzzy application, this work will provide strength for the spiritual muscles and courage for the struggle.'

Moody Monthly

'A tremendous exposition and splendid pastoral application.'

Trowel and Sword

Many thousands who did not share the advantage of the Westminster congregation will now have the privilege and joy of reading what they failed to hear.'

The Christian Herald

OLD TESTAMENT
EVANGELISTIC SERMONS

ISBN 0 85151 683 1
304 pp. Cloth-bound

'It is vintage wine indeed, and one could have wished for a volume twice the size. Can we expect more?'

Evangelical Presbyterian

'Nearly fifty years on, and the words are in cold print, yet they fire the soul! And surely that is why the book has been published . . . this book may help us to see how a greater mind than ours avoided the distractions and kept to the one great question . . . buy it! You will not be disappointed.'
'

Evangelical Action

EVANGELISTIC SERMONS
AT ABERAVON

ISBN 0 85151 362 X
308 pp. Large Paperback

'Early examples of that "logic-on-fire" which the author desired and commended to others. To me their abiding value lies in the intense seriousness of the preacher. They are worlds apart from the triviality of so much evangelism today.'

Dick Lucas in *The Churchman*

2 PETER

ISBN 0 85151 379 4
272 pp. Cloth-bound

A masterly example of the kind of expository preaching in popular vein that can result in the building up of a congregation in the Christian faith.'

Reformed Theological Review

'A model for preaching and . . . a storehouse of spiritual benefit.'

Ministry

D. MARTYN LLOYD-JONES: LETTERS 1919–1981
Selected with Notes by Iain H. Murray

ISBN 0 85151 674 2
270 pp. Cloth-bound

'Take this book reverently, and read to be enriched by the depth of spiritual insight and understanding which God graciously gave to his servant . . . Here is a book well-produced, lovely to handle, full of meaty subjects, with a good photograph of M.L.-J. on the dust-cover . . . it is well worth consideration as a "gift to a friend", but put one on your own shelf first!'

Reformed Theological Journal

AUTHORITY

ISBN 0 85151 386 7
96 pp. Paperback

'These are addresses given at a conference of students in 1957 and are still of superb value for students and young Christians . . . '

Vox Reformata

'This is a splendid introduction to the whole question of authority and may be studied with profit by the specialist or layman alike.'

The Gospel Magazine

KNOWING THE TIMES
Addresses delivered on Various Occasions
1942–1977

ISBN 0 85151 556 8
400 pp. Cloth-bound

'This is a most significant book . . . a challenge to return to Scripture, to stand by and for the gospel and to live to the glory of God.'

Evangelicals Now

'It ought to be read by every Christian leader. Highly recommended.'

Evangelical Action

'If I had my way, I would make sure that every potential candidate for the ministry not only read this book through, but also read it through regularly, at least once a year . . . probably one of the most significant of all the Lloyd-Jones works that has ever been published . . . it will give both encouragement and vision to those who are concerned with the cause of the gospel.'

The Churchman

WHAT IS AN EVANGELICAL?

ISBN 0 85151 626 2
80 pp. Paperback

'In characteristic style, Dr Lloyd-Jones offers a clear and succinct analysis of the theological trends within Evangelicalism . . . This must surely be one of the most useful books ever to come from Lloyd-Jones.'

Scottish Bulletin of Evangelical Theology

THE PURITANS:
THEIR ORIGINS AND SUCCESSORS

ISBN 0 85151 496 0
436 pp. Cloth-bound

'This book is hard to put down; it grips the reader and to it
he will want to return again and again. None can read it
without immense profit.'

Evangelical Times

For free illustrated catalogue please write to:
THE BANNER OF TRUTH TRUST
3 Murrayfield Road, Edinburgh EH12 6EL